T0341443

Reflections on the Folklife Festival

An Ethnography of Participant Experience

Special Publications of the Folklore Institute

Special Publications of the Folklore Institute is published at
Indiana University with the editorial guidance of the
Folklore Institute Faculty and Fellows. This series provide a
flexible forum for the occasional publication of reports on
current research, field data, bibliographies, course readings,
and other materials of interest to the broad folkloristic
community.

John H. McDowell, Editor
Inta Gale Carpenter, Associate Editor

Advisory Board
Richard Bauman

Mary Ellen Brown Dorothy Sara Lee
Sandra K. Dolby Warren E. Roberts
Hasan El-Shamy Gregory A. Schrempp
Henry Glassie Ronald R. Smith
Roger R. Janelli Beverly J. Stoeltje
John Wm. Johnson Ruth M. Stone

Reflections on the Folklife Festival

An Ethnography
of Participant Experience

Richard Bauman, Patricia Sawin, and Inta Gale Carpenter

WITH RICHARD ANDERSON, GARRY W. BARROW, WILLIAM J. WHEELER, AND JONGSUNG YANG

Special Publications of the Folklore Institute No. 2
Indiana University
BLOOMINGTON

ISBN: 1-879407-02-7 paper edition; 1-879407-03-5 cloth edition
Distributed by Indiana University Press,
Bloomington and Indianapolis

Printed in the United States of America

Contents

1.0 The Folklife Festival and the Problematics of Representation

A powerful stimulus to the politically informed and analytically self-conscious examination by folklorists and others of the problematics of representation has been the burgeoning of publicly oriented programs under the rubrics of folklore, folklife, or folk art (see e.g., Bauman and Sawin 1991; Camp and Lloyd 1980; Cantwell 1991a, 1991b; Feintuch 1988; Fine 1984; Kirshenblatt-Gimblett 1988, 1991; Kurin 1991; Seitel, 1991; Whisnant 1979, 1983).[1] As increasing numbers of academically trained folklorists have moved into extra-academic venues over the past two decades, they have inevitably employed presentational modes directed at different audiences and driven by different imperatives and standards from those in the academy. Prominent among these presentational—simultaneously representational—modes is the folklife festival.

The folklife festival is a modern form of cultural production (MacCannell 1976) which draws upon the building blocks and dynamics of such traditional events as festivals and fairs: complex, scheduled, heightened, and participatory events in which symbolically resonant cultural goods and values are placed on public display (Abrahams 1981; Stoeltje 1989). Folk festivals display forms of folk culture as conceived by folklorists and other cultural programmers and executed by practitioners they select.

The ideological foundation of contemporary American folklife festivals is a species of liberal pluralism, which promulgates a symbolically constructed image of the popular roots of American national culture by traditionalizing, valorizing, and legitimizing selected aspects of vernacular culture drawn from the diverse ethnic, regional, and occupational groups seen to make up American society. Folk culture is variously counterposed against elite, mass, or official culture as embodying values and social relations that are a necessary, natural, and valuable part of human existence, worthy of preservation and encouragement. The sometimes tacit, often explicit, assumption is that folk festivals can serve as instruments of such preservation and encouragement.

Folklorists are beginning to question, however, what the actual effects of such festive representations may be (see Camp and Lloyd 1980; Whisnant 1979; articles by McCarl, Santino, and Whisnant in Feintuch 1988). Thus far, much of this critical and reflexive examination of folklife festivals has been directed at the practice of the folklorists who stage them, questioning formerly tacit assumptions about the efficacy of festival representations toward the goal of maximizing the quotient of authenticity, accuracy, or verisimilitude. With few exceptions, the primary focus has been upon the actions of the folklorists themselves as agents within the larger social and political arena and the issues have been posed in terms of the degrees to which various modes of representation achieve the folklorists' agendas.[2] Little, if any, critical attention has focused on folklife festivals from the perspective of the participants themselves. In the following pages, we report on a project undertaken as a beginning toward filling this gap in our knowledge.

Those who champion the folklife festival as a form of representation often number among its virtues that it allows those whose culture is being represented far greater opportunity to talk back to the producers of the representation than is offered, say, by a published ethnography. This may be a potential of folklife festivals, to be sure, but it is rarely achieved in practice. Our project was motivated, in large part, by a concern to realize that potential. Still further, proponents of folklife festivals have insisted on the intellectual legitimacy of this mode of representation in the face of a tendency on the part of some academic scholars to disvalue it in favor of more conventional forms like the article or monograph. The legitimacy of these scholarly forms, however, depends significantly on openness to critique, not only by other scholars, but again, increasingly, by those who are the subjects of representation (see, e.g., Feld 1987; Mudimbe 1988). This essay, then, should also be seen in part as an attempt to fulfill that critical function for folklife festivals.

In practical terms, our project arose out of a convergence of interests between the Indiana University Folklore Institute and the Smithsonian Institution Office of Folklife Programs (OFP). At the time that the project took shape, in the fall of 1986, the OFP was engaged in a process of self-evaluation and the Festival of American Folklife (FAF)—as the activity that absorbs the lion's share of the program's energy and resources and the one for which it is best known—assumed a correspondingly central place in those deliberations. At the same time, the Folklore Institute was exploring ways to articulate the academic mission of the department with the interests of a significant number of graduate students in extra-academic careers. The plan for our ethnography of participant experience in the FAF emerged out of a series of discussions that fall and winter, first between Peter Seitel (then director of OFP) and Richard Bauman (then chair of the Folklore Institute), later involving other members of the respective institutions and still others working on the 1987 FAF. The project was jointly supported by the Folklore Institute, with special funds granted by the Indiana University Office of Research and Graduate Development, and the OFP, which contributed food and lodging during our stay in Washington.[3]

Fig. 1. Early moring at the 1987 Festival of American Folklife, Washington, D.C.
Photo: Richard Anderson

2.0 Introduction: An Ethnography of Participation in the 1987 Festival of American Folklife

Anyone who has worked in a festival will find much of our data familiar. Indeed, our initial interest was piqued by the anecdotes about festival successes and disasters circulating among folklorists who have worked as staff or volunteers at various folklife festivals. By the time the planning process ended, we took on the goal of attaining a new perspective on the familiar by seeking out experience from the participants' point of view, compiling our observations systematically, and analyzing them in terms of a unified theoretical frame.

The Festival of American Folklife, founded in 1967, has had an enormous influence on publicly oriented folklife programming in the United States, because of the scale and vigor of the festival, its location in the nation's capital, and the caliber of its staff. The festival has served as a training ground for many public-sector folklorists who have subsequently moved on to other positions around the country, and the FAF format has become a model for productions in many other locales. At the same time, it is necessary to keep in mind that the FAF carries a high level of prestige and therefore places personal and professional reputations (of the production and research staff as well as of the presenters and participants) under substantial scrutiny and risk.

2.1 Aspects of Festival Organization Pertinent to this Study

The FAF is usually organized into several distinct program areas; the specific programs vary from year to year, but typically include the presentation of the folk culture of a featured state and of a foreign country as well as an issue-oriented program (e.g., cultural conservation) and perhaps others (in 1987 the three program areas were: Michigan,

Washington, D.C. [instead of a foreign country], and "America's Many Voices" [language conservation]). Four main presentational foci for the festival have evolved over the years: musical and dance performance, occupational folklife (involving the representation of work skills), crafts demonstrations, and foodways (demonstration of the preparation of regional and ethnic dishes).

Participants involved in demonstrating crafts or occupational skills are usually provided with individual work stations where their tools and materials are set up and the products of their activity can be displayed. These participants have a definite place to belong amid the bustle of festival activity, but they are also expected to work more or less continuously throughout the festival day and to be prepared to answer questions at any time from the spectators who wander by and periodically gather around their demonstration areas. Craft demonstration areas are usually compact, with tables, work benches, and display racks for several participants grouped together under a large awning. Display areas for occupational skills can be large and spread-out and may include mock-ups of buildings, large machinery, and even an entire fishing boat, rodeo arena, or race track.

Foodways demonstrators, in contrast, rotate through the single demonstration kitchen in each program area, averaging one hour-long presentation per day. Spectators may drift in and out, but covered bleachers are provided to encourage an audience to stay for the entire demonstration. Musicians, similarly, usually give one formal, hour-long show per day on the large, elevated main stage which provides covered seating for an audience of 200 or more and serves as the organizational focus and most foregrounded display space in each program area. Main stage music is highly amplified, and the current performance can often be heard all over the program area and out onto the Mall beyond the festival.

Most participants are also asked to appear approximately once every other day on a "talk stage." The term is used to designate both the sites (low, tree-shaded stage platforms with gentle amplification and seating for no more than thirty to forty viewers) and the events that are held there, moderated discussions of the various skills on display and the social and cultural foundations of the various groups in which they are rooted. Talk stages frequently provide a comparative perspective by bringing together people from different cultural backgrounds who play the same instrument or practice similar crafts or occupations. The main themes for these presentations are worked out in advance, but the inspiration for specific topics and for the inclusion of specific participants often emerges during the course of the festival as presenters learn more about the pool of talent that has been assembled, especially about the relevant skills and interests that participants may have in addition to the specific ones that they have been invited to the festival to present.

All presentational formats featured at the festival (with the exception of most ongoing craft or occupational displays) are mediated by designated presenters, often, but not always, the fieldworkers who originally contacted and recruited particular performers for the festival. The presenters are usually academically trained folklorists, historians, museum specialists, or cultural programmers, who are charged with introducing and contextualizing the cultural forms on display, moderating discussion sessions, and serving as intermediaries between the festival producers and the participants. Some presenters have prior experience at serving in this capacity, and all receive briefings concerning what is expected of them shortly before the festival. Some fieldworkers, presenters, and staffers have the opportunity or desire to do more by way of preparing participants for the active reconceptualization of the activity they will present, some less. With this in mind, our research focused on exploring how the participants actually accommodate what they do to the complex representational demands of the staged event in which they are on display.

2.2 Research Design and Execution

Our analysis is based on data collected at and in connection with the 1987 FAF, primarily from a core group of about twenty participants in the Michigan program.[4] The project design (see appended "Research Guide") called for each of the six researchers from Indiana University, under the direction of Richard Bauman, to work closely with a small number of individual participants or groups.[5] The members of the research team were Richard Anderson, Garry Barrow, Inta Gale Carpenter, Patricia Sawin, William Wheeler, and Jongsung Yang.

While we attempted to document the experiences of a wide range of participants in terms of factors we anticipated would influence festival experience (see "Research Guide" sections 2.4 and 2.5), we should stress

Fig. 2. Videotaping activities and presentations   *Photo: Richard Bauman*

Fig. 3. Interviewing participants about developing impressions
Photo: Inta Gale Carpenter

that the selection of participants with whom we ultimately worked does not represent a systematic sample. We did work with: 1) both male and female participants [2.5c], 2) people of various ages (from late 20s to 60s) [2.5c], 3) people with a range of prior experience in public enactments (from none to considerable) [2.5a], 4) both those who were well known and those who were little known in their home communities prior to the festival [2.5b], 5) some participants who identified themselves strongly as representatives of a group or tradition and others who saw themselves primarily as individual artists [2.5d], and 6) participants in all four presentational categories (music, crafts, occupational folklife, and foodways) [2.4]. We were not able to include Black or Native American participants in our study, with the result that we have not covered variations in experience influenced by racial identification.

In most cases the researcher was able to travel to Michigan and interview chosen participants before the festival. We all spent the full two weeks at the 1987 FAF, living with the participants and staff and spending each day of the festival at the site on the Mall. Researchers documented the performances or demonstrations of the people with whom they were working, interacted with them informally on a daily basis, and conducted several interviews with them about their developing impressions of the festival. Afterwards, each researcher either travelled to Michigan again to conduct follow-up interviews or corresponded with the participants. Two researchers also observed the re-creation of the Michigan component of the FAF at the 1987 Festival of Michigan Folklife in East Lansing in August.

In the course of the festival several members of the research team also interacted informally with and consequently observed the reactions to the festival of several other Michigan participants[6] and several of the people from northwestern North Carolina who were participating in the "Cultural Conservation and Language" program.[7] In this report we occasionally refer to these other participants' impressions, especially when they appear to expand our picture of participant experience in significant dimensions.

During and after the festival the research team met frequently to coordinate efforts and ensure that we were collecting comparable data and producing complementary analyses. When the investigation was completed, each researcher submitted a report based on field notes, photographs, and audio- and videotape recordings. These served as the basis for the first draft of our festival ethnography (Sawin 1988), which we circulated to Smithsonian staff members, fieldworkers, and presenters involved in the Michigan display, from whom we sought comments and corrections. The present work incorporates this feedback, which at times amplified or corroborated our data, at other times offered productive corrections. References to and direct quotations from this dialogue have been worked into the body of the text or have been added as footnotes where appropriate.

2.3 A Reflexive Review of the Research Experience

To our knowledge, no one had previously attempted an ethnographic study of a folklife festival in progress. Certainly such an undertaking was unfamiliar to both the research team and the festival staff. This situation exerted particular stresses on researchers, staff, and participants in ways that influenced the research process, the activities of both staff and participants during the festival, and consequently the data we collected and our interpretations of it. Our presence added another factor to the already complex situation to which staff and participants had to adapt. We urge readers to bear that influence in mind. The specific influences that we have been able to trace or about which we have been told are described below.

2.3.1 Relationship between Researchers and Staff. The plan for research had been worked out jointly between Richard Bauman and Peter Seitel. Only after the project was well underway, as we became aware of tensions between various levels in the festival hierarchy and between the OFP staff in Washington and fieldworkers in Michigan, did we realize we had somewhat naively assumed that directorial permission implied universal consent. In retrospect, we recognize ways we could have more actively promoted a collegial dialogue around what we believe is common cause.

It was our perception that many staff members and presenters (in addition to resenting us as an intrusion authorized from above) tended to understand our involvement in the festival in one of two ways.[8] Some staff members evidently believed we were there to evaluate them (not unreasonably, given that granting agencies commonly send another folklorist to evaluate festivals they have supported). Evaluation was not our intention or goal. We recognize, however, that in observing participants, we necessarily subjected the staff members and especially the presenters to unusual and unexpected scrutiny and that the perceived presence of "evaluators" added to everyone's stress level and may thus have exacerbated some of the problems we observed.

Second, some of the fieldworkers/presenters worried that our interest in interviewing people with whom they were engaged in ongoing research might upset a delicate research situation or in some other way hamper work-in-progress. This imposed additional limitations on our choice of participants and in later stages sometimes steered our interest away from the concrete effects of festival involvement on participants' subsequent lives (which would have required more extensive follow-up fieldwork), enhancing our focus instead on the participants' intellectual and emotional adaptation during the festival. Perceptions of suspicion and hostility toward us during the festival (to cite the extreme example, being addressed as "carpetbaggers") certainly increased our own stress level and occasionally encouraged us to conceptualize certain relationships in adversarial terms. Furthermore, our presence necessarily introduced an additional element into the evolving relationship between participant and presenter, and in at least one instance a presenter communicated to us afterwards that the researcher's frequent presence had "complicated [her] interaction with both the participants and the Smithsonian staff," possibly interfering with her bonding with the people she was presenting (Gilmore, correspondence, 4-27-89, p.3).

2.3.2 Perspectival Bias. In a fundamental way, this report provides a biased account. But this *perspectival* bias was built in consciously and from the beginning; we deliberately oriented our investigation toward the perspective of the performers and demonstrators. Given our approach, others involved with the 1987 FAF have challenged the validity of our results; reactions to our draft proposal (Sawin 1988) included, for example: "I feel the report suffers from its lack of systematic attention to the role and perspectives of the organizers" (Sommers, correspondence, 8-31-88, p. 1); "A full ethnography and understanding of participant experience would depend heavily on knowing the experiences of people in the other groups as well" (Spitzer, personal communication). We continue to believe that our selective orientation was warranted, all the more so because what the participants *perceived* to be happening did not always coincide with what the festival organizers intended or even with what they had explicitly communicated. Additionally, we chose to foreground the participants' experience because up to the point of our research it had taken a back seat to the concerns of festival producers and folklorists who analyzed how folklife festivals worked from *their* perspectives. Still, we acknowledge that our decision to focus on the participants has influenced our report in at least three ways.

First, our lack of communication with staff increased tensions between the two groups. Second, we were little more clear than were the participants regarding where various staff members stood amidst a complex of overlapping responsibilities, affiliations, and hierarchies of control and decision making. As a result, as Janet Gilmore has pointed out to us, our use of the term "staff" is somewhat loose (4-27-89, p. 3). In the marked sense, we have used "staff" to refer to folklorists, or those designated as such, employed by the OFP for the long-term planning of this festival and have correspondingly specified "presenters," "fieldworkers," and "production staff" or "design staff" when those particular groups were involved. However, we also use "staff" in an unmarked sense to include all the above (non-exclusive) categories either when all are involved or (as was often the case) when participants were not aware of the precise position of the staff members with whom they were dealing.

Third, several festival organizers suggested that in earlier versions of this ethnography our attempt to interpret data collected only from the participants' restricted perspective led us to "attribute motives" to staff members. We subsequently have tried to correct such speculation. We are concerned here to represent the experience of the participants, in full awareness that producers or staffers or presenters may well have intended or experienced or interpreted things differently—indeed, we would expect so. We also recognize that those who work closely with the participants are generally aware of the challenges and difficulties posed by the festival and the participants' abilities to adapt.

2.3.3 Relationship between Researchers and Participants. We also anticipated and, in reviewing our data, have noted increasingly that our presence as researchers added yet more confusion and yet another role as "object of study" to the repertoire of possibilities for the participants with whom we worked (see section 3.3.1 on roles). Some of them had been interviewed in Michigan before the festival and therefore had anticipated that another researcher (other than the one who originally contacted them to come to the FAF) would be talking with them again in D.C. Some we contacted only at the festival. Most did not form a clear notion of where we fit into the staff hierarchy nor of how or where the observations we were gathering would be used (both Gilmore [4-27-89, p. 3] and Sommers [8-31-88, p. 2] emphasized participant confusion about us in their responses to the first report).

Reactions varied. Two participants dubbed Richard Anderson "the spy," mostly as a friendly joke, but also as an indicator of confusion and genuine unease and as a means of seeking clarification from presenters and others about just what we were doing.[9] In reflexive jest, Raymond Leslie, observing Lewis VanBuskirk eating an ice cream cone while talking to Inta Carpenter, inquired if his ice cream cone were a microphone. When Steve Jayton was asked to be observed during the FAF and later interviewed about his festival experience, there was a telling split-second pause and a change in tone of voice before his affirmative answer.

Participants made sense—and use—of us in multiple ways. At times they turned to us for various kinds of pragmatic support during the course of a routine day on the Mall, at others we served as sounding boards as they puzzled out definitions for their activities, at still others we were convenient sympathetic listeners for their complaints and requests for changes or improvements. The roles into which they cast us suggest further ways in which we affected our own data. In at least one instance, we suspect that the researcher may have influenced the participants' decisions about their performance tactics in a fairly direct fashion. Garry Barrow worked with the Simons, who have a family string band. He videotaped several of their performances and on the first night of the festival played back the tape of their first performance. He notes, "As they watched, they remarked on how the audience responded to various numbers, and decided that the fiddle tunes were consistently met with the greatest enthusiasm" and "my general impression is that whenever audience response began to sag, the Simons would fall back on 'Orange Blossom Special' or some similar upbeat instrumental." In a more diffuse sense, too, it is likely that our attention and questioning increased the participants' awareness of their adjustment process.

Most importantly, the reader should bear in mind that many of our insights inevitably have been generated around problems and points of friction and indeterminacy. Reflexivity is heightened in situations of unfamiliarity or moments of crisis, as those involved examine and evaluate what has been going on in the search for a course of action. Any apparently negative cast to segments of this report is an artifact of the situations in which participants were most strongly motivated to share their impressions with us and of our attempt to zero in on the points at which participants had to do the most work, where their agency was at its most vigorous.

3.0 Participant Experience: Diverse and Negotiated Agendas and Understandings

In planning this research we aimed to document the range of experiences that participants in the 1987 FAF would have and we anticipated that their experiences would vary according to the type of activity presented, their prior experience with self-presentation, their visibility in the home community, gender, age, and degree of self-identification as representative of a group or tradition (as opposed to as an individual artist). We also recognized that the requirement to re-present or re-create for an audience behaviors that have their primary existence in other social settings could be a significant factor in participants' responses to the festival. Our research revealed, however, that the necessity of making the kinds of practical and intellectual readjustments required by the festival frame assumed even more prominence than we had expected.

The fluid and negotiable nature of what it means to participate in a folklife festival would seem to provide significant openings for creativity and to allow participants an opportunity to influence and shape how they are presented to the public. But the necessary fluidity, especially of a large and complex festival such as the FAF, could also be the source of confusions and negative experiences. Perhaps inevitably, given the variety of theoretical approaches current in the discipline of folklore, curatorial staff, production staff, and presenters differ among themselves over definitions of "folklore" and the purposes of a festival. Participants who received instructions from several different staff members not infrequently felt that they were getting conflicting messages about what they should do and how they would contribute to a "folklife festival." Similarly, the variety of activities currently included in the FAF made it difficult for the participants to deduce any consistent definition from observing their fellows. To add yet another element to an already complex picture, participants were likely to have their own notions influenced by contact with jamborees, bluegrass or other music festivals.

In our work, we observed how participants wrestle with their own and others' definitions as they come to terms with a basic contextualizing question, one that lies at the heart of frame analysis—"What is it that is going on here?"(on frame analysis see Goffman 1974). We witnessed how participants arrive at differential and shifting understandings that require constant work to achieve, sustain, and revise. Much of the effort required of participants goes toward working out these frames in their own minds, negotiating and testing them in interactions with fellow participants, audience, and staff, and enacting or embodying them in their daily presentations. Participants' responses to the festival, their conclusions about what they are doing (and what they are *supposed* to be doing) in this novel situation, and the resulting performances emerged out of the participants' own agendas, expectations, and past experience in festivals and other display events (or lack thereof), and were influenced by input from festival organizers and by the unfolding of the festival itself—the space, the ambience, the audience, other participants, and staff.

Although most participants feel confident about their ability to perform the task or art they have been asked to display, the unfamiliar requirements of festival re-presentation make them feel at risk. Most are little prepared for what will happen and need guidance (or at least some time on the Mall) in order to figure out how best to transform their everyday activities into a recontextualized presentation or enactment for a festival audience. People may well not be especially reflective about their everyday activities, but they are forced to reflect when asked to re-present that activity in the context of a festival. Under these unusual circumstances the participants with whom we worked found that they needed a more conscious concept of what it was they did at home in order to readapt that for this new context. But adapting oneself to the requirements of festival re-presentation, an inevitable component of festival participation, is by no means necessarily a negative experience. At least one participant whom we interviewed, Steve Jayton, regarded his own grappling with a more conscious understanding of what he was about as one of the benefits of the festival.

From the perspective of many participants, staff instructions did not deal sufficiently with the practical and conceptual questions of what they were actually supposed to do in front of an audience or how they could understand themselves as fitting into the FAF. (The participant handbook and the participants' orientation session concentrated on the practical aspects of living while at the festival: how to get there, how to do laundry, where to eat, when one will be paid, and so on.) Participants' needs in this area varied considerably depending on their self-concept and temperament and on the nature of the activity to be re-presented. For fiddler Ray Leslie the problem was mostly philosophical. Prior to the festival, Leslie received messages that seemed conflicting and which confused his sense of the philosophical base and artistic standards of the festival. The Smithsonian staff asked him to emphasize the older tunes in his repertoire, but then (as he understood it) objected to hammered dulcimer player Gil Pauley, who usually accompanied him on those pieces, as a revivalist.[10]

For commercial fisherman Will Ralston, in contrast, the frustrations were more practical, focusing on attaining a sufficient understanding of expectations, resources, and possibilities to enable him to do the best possible job of representing and explaining his profession. Ralston had never been to a festival, although he had talked about fishing and given presentations to the Lions' Club. But his previous audiences had a pretty good idea of what fishing was about. He really did not know what to expect in D.C. The Smithsonian staff had told him, he reported, that they would like him to make a net and talk. He asked what he should bring to display, whether he could hang things up, how big the storage area was, but did not remember getting clear answers. He was sent a layout plan, but not consulted on the set-up of the display; and after arriving on site, he felt that the display needed more pictures so that people could understand what they were talking about and that a pond could have been built a couple of feet deep, so they could put a 12-foot or 16-foot boat in it and simulate the raising of a net. Many different people had called him in Michigan but none seemed to know anything about commercial fishing. One day someone called to ask if he could smoke fish. He said he could. He then was asked if he might help participants from the Upper Peninsula smoke fish in a refrigerator. Aghast at using a refrigerator, Ralston explained that when people smoke for themselves they each have their own way, but he felt he was not being understood.

g. 4   Preparing to smoke fish in a refrigerator   *Photo: Richard Anderson*

Thus from the very beginning of the interaction with festival staff, ιere is potential for confusion. The participants recognize that they ave been hired or commissioned to represent something by people ιey perceive as relatively well-educated (and yet who sometimes dem- nstrate odd gaps in knowledge, as the example with the smoking ιggested to Ralston), but who do not fully articulate the standards they ave in mind nor engage in a thorough dialogue with the people they ιtrust with the representation of tradition.

In the process of achieving their day-to-day activity at the festival, ιrticipants found themselves grappling with multiple issues all at once. ι an effort to clarify this presentation, we have identified four basic sues or questions that appeared to serve as foci for negotiation:

1) Why should I participate? (personal agendas)
2) What is the Smithsonian?
3) What is my role vis à vis the staff?
4) What is it that I am engaged in? (framing)

Readers will recognize, however, that these issues are very much inter-twined in participants' experience and that distinguishing them is simply a heuristic device.

3.1 Why Should I Participate? (Personal Agendas)

An invitation to participate in the Smithsonian's festival is usually perceived as a great compliment and offers participants an opportunity to travel, receive recognition for their skills, and engage in a variety of new activities. Most participants were aware and appreciative of the honor being paid them. Steve Jayton spoke of being asked to come to the festival as "the honor of a lifetime," and Ray Leslie said, "Just being invited was enough." In an early interview, Will Davis commented, "I felt honored to be invited to come, and you know an opportunity like that only comes along once in a while." After two weeks at the festival, his positive feelings had only intensified: "If nobody for the rest of my life ever told me I did a good job at anything, enough people told me while I was here these two weeks that I'd be set." ("People" here meant the public.)

At least some of the participants agreed to be in the festival because they *also* had specific individual agendas above and beyond promoting or publicizing their skill or tradition and because they anticipated that going to Washington would provide certain benefits and enable them to accomplish their own goals. Many realized that participation would not be an unmitigated benefit, for it would require a substantial amount of work and, sometimes, significant financial sacrifices.[11] Therefore, the perception of the festival as an occasion to promote personal agendas in part compensated for such liabilities.

Several of the participants with whom we worked were interested in the specifically *political* potential of coming to Washington, D.C., a place they equated with access to powerful people, and by association, viewed as a means by which to enhance their own power and influence or to further political causes important to them. Among the commercial fishermen, Will Ralston told Richard Anderson during an interview several weeks before the festival that he would have to take off work, but thought it would be worthwhile because of the opportunity to educate potentially influential people about "a hotly debated" issue in Michigan: gill net fishing, which is now illegal except for some Native Americans.

River guide Will Davis inquired about how to get in touch with lobby-ists, because he was concerned about legislation that affects his business, specifically laws that limit the size and type of fish that his clients can catch. Harry Elder hoped to influence public opinion for the repeal of a ban on the sale of muskrat meat in Michigan and even indicated after the festival that he probably would not have gone except for that opportunity. He and his wife perceived that their own power would be temporarily enhanced through their association with the festival and the fact that they were acting *in* Washington, D.C. The Elders opened their first show by giving pro-rat t-shirts to representatives from the Michigan governor's office.

Several participants were actively transforming the recognition ac-corded festival participation into tangible goals related to *personal career and economic advancement*. Karl Arnold, viewing himself as a representative of Ukrainian folk art and culture, hoped national recognition would earn him the respect of a few older Ukrainian embroiderers, who, in turn, would let him interview them and document their collections and patterns. His long-term goal was to obtain federal and state grant support for documentation projects, a goal he has realized subsequent to the festival.

Fishing guide Will Davis came because it was a once-in-a-life-time opportunity both as honor (see above) *and* as business. He prominently displayed his business cards beside a photo album of his various guiding trips, thus transforming a demonstration space into a promotional space. When a special evening event on the Mall with Smithsonian museum "Associates" was threatened by rain and participants were transported back to the hotel, Davis and others expressed frustration at the missed opportunity to meet people perceived to be influential friends of the Smithsonian" and potential clients. In this situation, the Smithsonian turned out to be less of a patron than expected.

Steve Jayton voiced two main agendas, to *promote his state* and to get a lot of *work* done on the boat he was building. It had been sold for two years and he was using the weeks at the FAF to finish it. (He also had a very practical concern: getting it built up enough so that he could safely trailer it home.) Promoting the state he loves presented little problem. Various signs, including the insignia burned onto the boat, indicated that his primary loyalty was to Michigan rather than to the FAF: "Con-structed in Washington, D.C., June 24–July 5, 1987, for the Michigan Sesquicentennial by Steve Jayton and Will Davis, #34."

Jayton's second goal—to finish the boat—sometimes came into conflict with the kind of presentation he felt the Smithsonian expected and which he wanted to offer, for during critical stages, such as gluing, he had to ignore people and work. In the second week as the tasks at hand required increasing concentration, Steve and Will would arrive at the festival site before it opened in order to work without the distraction of an audience, thereby denying altogether the frame of demonstration (we will take up the issue of framing and frame conflicts in section 3.4).

Jayton also forfeited an important personal goal. He had originally planned to involve his daughter in building the boat so that she could perfect her knowledge of the skill and in turn start teaching her son. She could not accompany Jayton to Washington and since everyone "told me I'd be crazy not to go," he delayed the process of passing on the

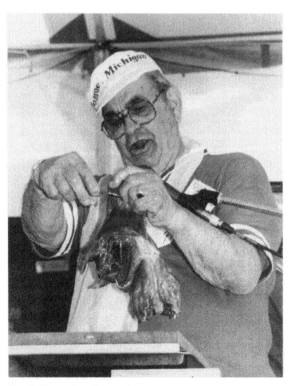

Fig. 5   Preparing the muskrat   *Photo: Patricia Sawin*

g. 6   Boat insignia promoting Michigan at the FAF   *Photo: Inta Gale Carpenter*

mily's traditional occupation. On the other hand, festival participa-
on enabled Will Davis, a younger, though very accomplished, boat
uilder, to pick up some "little tricks and techniques" from Jayton.

Many of the participants were explicit about having a *tourist agenda*.
uite a few were in D.C. for the first time and might never have the
pportunity to come again. When the hotel, however, proved to be
eyond walking distance to Washington sites and the metro, especially
r older participants from rural backgrounds, seemed daunting, some
ied to compensate creatively (e.g., Polly Elder asking Patricia Sawin to
ay postcards for her in the museums so she would have something to
nd to her friends). Quite a few of the participants actively sought, or
ished for, opportunities to break frame by becoming tourists at the
stival, not tourist attractions. Steve Jayton and Will Davis worked out
ime off" between themselves, and Will commented positively on what
had seen (and learned) from the others.

Performers were more free than demonstration people to sightsee,
pecially to visit the museums encircling the Mall, and spoke of these
portunities as highlights of the trip. The opportunity to visit famous

sites, for example, promised status back home. At the social one night, Rose Jenner announced, "I've been to see Rembrandt and Renoir, Monet and Manet." She had also visited the Wyeth series on Helga at the National Gallery, and although she hadn't heard of Wyeth before, she now "knew all about him and Helga." She liked the Impressionists "very much," but she wished she could have seen something "like the Mona Lisa that everyone back home has heard about."

Ray Leslie, according to his wife Rowena, needed to get over an inferiority complex about his playing, and *her* agenda was that the festival experience would provide him concrete evidence of his expertise. Their shared agenda was to promote his particular Michigan style of "playable, danceable music." They know, however, that promoting the music in the form they want is dependent on personal contact and encouragement *in situ*. Thus, in terms of *their* musical agenda, the FAF stage never could approximate performance contexts typical for Ray— the jamboree or dance. Ray appeared on stage alone, and while he devoted himself whole-heartedly to his playing, he was unable to establish intimacy with the constantly changing audience, who did not respond with the accustomed enthusiasm.* This situation increased his anxiety over ability. When the talk stage was canceled one rainy day, he interpreted it personally, by speculating that he "hadn't been good enough" and that the Smithsonian, finding him expendable, had canceled his appearance. In this defensive moment, he then proceeded to criticize the festival staff, for real and imagined slights.**

* The selection process for the FAF perhaps weighs against "the gentle performers" and tips toward the more flashy ones whose music readily catches the attention of and is accessible to the large and general festival audiences: "To the end, I expressed resistance to including them—if for no other reason than the fact that I had seen what 'gentle' [the unembellished playing of well-known parlor/dance tunes, in a technique that involves minimal arm movement in bowing and a soft sound quality] performances produce in festival audiences and wanted to save them the embarrassment they did indeed encounter" (Tom Vennum, personal communication).

** "In addressing the experiences and opinions of the participants, you have invaluably called attention to many of the slights they suffer from the various festival staffs and procedures, the worst one of which appears to be a lack of recognition of participants as equal, capable human beings with valid and complex emotional responses to co-workers and events" (Gilmore, 4-27-89, p. 3). "Whatever their personal feeling about the particular traditions selected, staff members must

Eventually Leslie did enjoy himself, largely because of the ties he established with fellow musicians and the opportunity to jam with them. He received tremendous personal validation ("the thrill of my life") when one of the Michigan groups invited him to join them in performing their "Anglo-French String Band" music on the large evening dance party stage. At the end of two weeks, Rowena Leslie said that her agenda for Ray had been accomplished.

Participants in the FAF arrive hoping for professional visibility and recognition; they expect to lobby legislators, to network on behalf of personal ambitions, to be tourists, to find personal identity, or actually to finish a job. Our observations of the multiple and varied agendas with which the participants arrive at the festival strongly suggest that the event can neither contain, anticipate, nor fully satisfy all the expectations it arouses and that at the time of the festival, some of these personal agendas—and the frustration, anxiety, or fatigue associated with them—overshadow the overall thrill and honor of being invited and featured. More positive reactions reassert themselves as the festival experience recedes and is recalled in retrospect (see 4.0, below).

3.2 What Is the Smithsonian?

The Smithsonian's reputation precedes it, which is, in part, why an invitation to participate in "the Smithsonian Institution's Festival of American Folklife" is so readily perceived as a mark of prestige and honor. Few participants, however, have any clear conception of the relation of the Office of Folklife Programs to the rest of the Institution, which leaves room for participants to make and act on unspoken assumptions. Harry and Polly Elder anticipated dealing with what they termed a "top of the line

---

be encouraging to participants. There is something to be said for the insincere, bubbleheaded enthusiastic act put on by some of the Michigan Festival organizers for making performers feel wanted" (FAF fieldworker, personal communication). Janet Gilmore reported that two of the commercial fishermen for whom she was presenter similarly felt anxiety over what they perceived as a lack of attention from the staff members with whom they had previous contact: "I recall Richards and Ray both feeling rejected . . . during the first days of the festival: courted from afar by regular phone calls . . . , Richards and Ray had trouble not receiving the same kind of attention from them at the festival and accepting me (the presenter) as their substitute" (Gilmore, 4-17-89, p. 9).

institution." When they discovered on the day before opening that the demonstration kitchen was not ready, they experienced considerable anxiety,[12] not so much because they would have been unable to adapt, but rather because their sense of the entire operation was momentarily threatened. Similarly, upon arriving in D.C., Karl Arnold readjusted his previous expectations: "I'll be honest with you. [I thought,] 'This is a BIG thing.' Fine. It's a big thing. The impression I was left with was that the entire Mall would be exhibits—wall to wall exhibits. When we were flying in I said, 'Oh, they've already got *some* of the tents up.'" To his subsequent surprise, he learned that *all* the tents were already up.

Participants seem to construct an image of the Smithsonian based on their own experiences and interests. Arnold's collection of Ukrainian embroidery contains what he considers "museum pieces." Assuming that he was dealing with a portion of the Smithsonian *museum*, Arnold had brought (and re-ironed) trunks full of embroidery, which he expected to display in glass museum cases (as at other festivals).[13]

The Simons and other musicians, on the other hand, conceived of the Smithsonian in terms of concerts and stages, and as performers, they expected a quiet dressing room where they could tune their instruments, stretch out their vocal chords, go over numbers, relax between performances, and prepare themselves psychologically for the audience. Since, as Mike Simon put it, "The first set is your *only* set," such a warm-up place seemed essential to the participants who want to put their best foot forward. Bob Jameson, in contrast, found his expectations fulfilled. Accustomed to doing demonstrations in similar circumstances at small festivals and trade shows, he had honed his "checklist of tools and materials down to a science" and was impressed with FAF organization, which he found more efficient and responsive than at other demonstration sites he had experienced.

3.3 What Is My Role Vis-à-vis the Staff?

3.3.1 Artist, worker, guest? Since participants are initially unclear about what "participating in a folklife festival" entails (a topic we will take up again in section 3.4, below), they are also often unsure of what their role is relative to the festival staff. Are they guests, or hired workers, or honored artists? Part of the beauty of the festival experience is, of course, that some of these hierarchical distinctions can be abrogated. Participants and presenters who already knew each other well often worked as egalitarian teams. Several participants spoke warmly of the friendships they had developed during the days on the Mall with volunteers (e.g., Will Davis and Steve Jayton came to rely on their volunteer to answer the repetitive questions and cover for them when they both took breaks).

Still, participants seem to have encountered inconsistent messages about roles from interactions with staff, presenters, and fieldworkers in the course of the festival (and the planning period), which meant that they sometimes had to switch roles or add unexpected ones, or that they found assigned roles restricting or inconsistent with their self-image. Karl Arnold was typical of many participants in perceiving himself as a self-sufficient sort of person, capable of taking care of his own needs. At the beginning of the week, he discovered that he needed a windscreen, but the presenter, whose assigned duty it was to meet such unanticipated needs, had so many other roles to fill he couldn't provide the equipment in a timely fashion. Arnold was prevented from doing so himself because of *his role as artist*. Without the necessary materials, however, Arnold couldn't fully demonstrate his egg-decorating skills until the middle of the week, and thus was doubly-denied. He couldn't demonstrate his own resourcefulness, nor could he excel in his effectively restricted role as master craftsman for lack of the proper equipment.

The two evening receptions proved particularly ambiguous with regard to clear role definitions. Participants were *invited* to attend, which seemed to emphasize the definition of them as guests of the Smithsonian. However, these evenings also seemed to be obligatory, suggesting that attendance was part of what one was required to do as a sort of employee of the festival. But if participants were required to attend, were they to be paid? ("It wasn't in my contract," one participant noted.)

These special events generated talk during meals, spreading the confusion and perhaps a touch of resistance, among presenters as well as participants.* While participants with political agendas or market agendas redefined obligation as opportunity, others wondered, "Why can't those people come when everyone else does?", raising questions of status and hierarchy. At least some participants were embarrassed to attend a reception and interact on an even footing with the Smithsonian

---

*Janet Gilmore reports: "Presenters hotly protested the lack of adequate disclosure . . . ; there was some interest in boycotting the event" (4-27-89, p. 1).

Associates without going back to the hotel to shower and change clothes after a long, sweaty day on the Mall. Steve Jayton summed up the ambiguity when he commented that he did not intend to work all day on the boat he was building in his coat and tie.

3.3.2 Hierarchies of Relating. An endemic feature of the FAF as presently constituted is that there are relatively large numbers of people involved with the festival—presenters, curatorial staff, production staff and OFP officials (plus fieldworkers at an earlier stage)—all of whom are empowered (tacitly, explicitly, or effectively) to make theoretical and practical decisions that affect the participants.* The profusion of authorities, the chains of information-flow and decision-making are possibly no more obvious to the staff than to the participants, but they are clearly bewildering to the participants with definite repercussions. During any given day, participants may interact with the director of the OFP, the director of the festival, the curator of the Michigan section, the coordinator of the Michigan section, the director of the presenters, the director of the site, presenters (not restricted to those with whom they were officially working), and volunteers, with each giving reactions, advice, and commentary, sometimes in highly, if unintentionally, contradictory fashion.

The lack of clarity apparent to participants stems at least in part from the involvement of so many knowledgeable people, each of whom perceives valid intellectual and practical reasons for wanting presentations to be conducted in particular ways.** From the participants' point of

* "In view of how baffled I remain about the Smithsonian and festival production staff hierarchy, and how confused I was about which staff person had what responsibilities during the festival planning process—they all asked the same kinds of questions about prospective participants, props, siting problems, and events and presumably they approached participants in the same manner—I think all newcomers, presenters and participants alike could have done with a flow chart of Smithsonian and festival production personnel (with their responsibilities well designated), a visit to the OFP, and an explanation of where the folklife program fits in the Smithsonian" (Gilmore, 4-27-89, p. 9).

* * "Some staff administrators have training in folklore, ethnography and representation. Some staff folklorists have administrative experience and experience in genres of presentation. Among staff of either background, disagreements often arise from the administrator who is beyond her/his ability on content or from the scholar who is disengaged from problems of production and representation. Unevenness in training, experience and motivation leads to the profusion of authorities you note. The OFP public self-image of its social structure—a sort of sixties-era 'We are all in this program together'—combined with academic

ew, however, what this boils down to is that there are many different
eople giving orders and directions about the same matters and that it is
ften difficult to figure out to whom one should go for information, or
hose information is definitive.

Such a situation favored those participants who were accompanied
y a fieldworker/presenter with few other duties and strong prior loyal-
es to the same tradition and to the people themselves (for example,
ennis Au with the Elders, Glenn Hinson with the people from North
arolina) and who could run interference for them. Note that in this
istance the value of the presenter to the participant in accomplishing
le festival recontextualization merges with his/her taking care of prac-
cal difficulties, thereby leaving participants free to sustain the presen-
tion frame themselves.

4   What Is It that I Am Engaged In? (Framing)

3.4.1 Framing, Participant Solutions. Participants in the FAF are invited
• the festival because they have expertise in a particular skill or perfor-
ance genre. Musicians and dancers are then asked to "perform," while
iose involved in crafts, foodways, and occupational activities are asked to
lemonstrate," with the presenter aiding "the 'non-performer' partici-
ints in material, occupational and culinary demonstrations [to] present
e nature and meaning of their activity so that it becomes a performance"
pitzer 1987:10,14). Depending upon the type of activity to be presented
id upon the individuals involved, there is usually more than one possible
ay for participants to construe "what it is that's going on here." Lacking
ther explicit re-contextualizing instructions or adequate and concrete
planations of "folklife" and "festival," participants frequently need to
define what they are doing in terms of some intuitively understood
tivity in which they feel they could appropriately be involved. Frequent
iswers to the basic question, "what does my activity here count as an
stance of?", included (in addition to demonstration and performance)
ork, display, instruction, exhibition, and various combinations or "lami-
itions" of these (for example, a demonstration of a performance) (Goffman
'74:82,156ff.).

<hr>

•tions of individual intellectual freedom and politically sensitive issues of
tonomy for people claiming special 'community-insider' knowledge—keep
iims to authority rather diffuse (personal communication, festival organizer)."

The *performance* frame involves an assumption of accountability to an audience for an authoritative display of communicative competence, subject to evaluation for the relative skill and effectiveness with which the act of communication is accomplished, above and beyond its informational content (Bauman 1977). *Demonstration*, by contrast, is a representational frame in which "a tasklike activity" is done "out of its usual functional context in order to allow someone who is not the [demonstrator] to obtain a close picture of the doing of the activity" (Goffman 1974:66). Some demonstrations may be framed as *instruction*, in which the purpose is to teach the observer how a task is accomplished. While performance, demonstration, and instruction focus as much or more on process as on product, *exhibition* displays products, objects. Thus, some craftspeople, taking account of the circumstance that the FAF is an activity of the nation's most prominent museum and understanding museums to be in the business of exhibiting objects, brought special objects of their own to exhibit in their work areas. *Work* is a frame in which the carrying out of a task for its usual functional purpose is the dominant consideration, without direct regard for an observing audience.

It may be well to emphasize again that frames, as we use the notion, represent participant orientations to situations. Frames may be relatively clear and stable or they may be ambiguous and shifting. They may be shared or held differentially. They seldom, if ever, occur singly, but are combined in shifting hierarchies of dominance. It is also significant that festival, in its essence, is set apart from everyday life. Festivity is a form of play in which work is either backstaged or markedly reframed to be consistent with the overarching play frame of the festival itself (see Stoeltje 1989).

Those participants who, for a variety of reasons, were able to figure out and sustain a simple, but flexible interpretation of what they were doing generally felt most comfortable and most satisfied with their participation. Participants who remained unsure about what it was that they were doing, or who reached conclusions at odds with those they perceived the staff to hold, frequently felt out-of-sync with the proceedings and were dissatisfied with the quality of their presentation or with their treatment by the Smithsonian. It is important to recognize, as we will stress below and return to in section 3.4.5, that every participant felt that his/her reputation was on the line (i.e., that they were all "performing" in that sense) and that rapid shifts from one role to another,

g. 7   Making wooden shoes   *Photo: Patricia Sawin*

activities that had to be sustained despite the lack of adequate materials or tools or space, and requests to perform activities for which the participant had not been able to prepare sufficiently all threatened a participant's face in significant ways.

"Demonstration" seems to be the interpretive frame most frequently invoked by the participants. All of these activities are recontextualized within the festival and thus become representations or demonstrations of the activity as it would occur in its usual context under normal circumstances. Even the main-stage performances are at least perfunctorily framed as demonstrations of performance (because the presenter introduces the act by talking about the culture the performers come from, which is precisely the sort of information that the usual audience for that performance genre would *not* need). And for participants, the most obvious way to re-adapt their usual activities for public presentation appears to have been to add more explanation and try to adopt an instructional mode. Still, "performance" and various varieties of "work" were also easily available as frames that could be combined with or conflict with the underlying idea of demonstrating.

Understanding one's activity as a demonstration worked well for many of the people whom we studied. In contrast especially to the performance frame, the demonstration frame is relatively forgiving. Participants and presenters engaged in a demonstration explicitly recognize that they are to treat the process as engaged in ordinarily as a routine or scenario to be replayed in slow motion, dissected, expanded, and annotated. Demonstrators can talk about the fact that they are not able to do whatever they are doing quite as they would at home, which provides a built-in excuse for failures. It is understood that adaptations have had to be made—unusual cookware used to facilitate display, smaller batches prepared, ingredients substituted, seasonal foods cooked out of season—so that explaining the cultural conversion is an expected part of the demonstration. Thus, to cite one example, the unavailability of rutabagas for pasty-making in D.C. became a resource for appropriate on-stage talk (comparison and discussion) rather than a performance-dooming lack (as it would be in the performance frame). (Both on-and off-stage, it also became a resource for joking, relaxing, and even bonding: D.C. can't be either as important or as daunting as imagined if you can't buy rutabagas here, while shared narratives about the miraculous last minute saves contributed to feelings of camaraderie among the interacting individuals.)

To put it another way, demonstrators *are* performers as well, since they are talking and acting in front of an audience, though without the degree of accountability that performance demands, especially since their activity frame not only sustains, but also actually encourages maneuvers that would constitute a frame-break for a pure performance.

Moreover, it is a significant aspect of many craft, occupational, and foodways demonstrations at the festival that the attention span of the audience members, the limited time available for certain demonstrations (principally foodways), and other practical considerations means that the *products* of the tasks on display are not always completed or available during the demonstration itself. Thus, we have food preparation without finished dishes, fishing demonstrations without fish, furniture carving without completed tables or chairs, and so on. The result, then, must be demonstrations of process without product, a focus on the task rather than on the result for which the task is usually done and by which it is evaluated. While this might be mitigated by accompanying displays of products or outcomes, the special nature of festival enactments before audiences makes demonstrations of process an adaptive mode of representation.

People who first became comfortable in the relaxed frame of demonstration could sometimes slip frame and, leaving behind their self-conscious amateur theatrical status, enter into that enviable realm (from an actor's standpoint) where displayed enactment and real activity merge. Steve Jayton got so wrapped up in one of his "stream-side cooking" demonstrations that he instinctively turned to rinse his hands in the (non-existent) stream. As Polly Elder gained confidence in her presentational skills, she became increasingly animated and playful. At one level she became more aware of the audience as people she could perform to, play up to, and entertain with her contextualizing stories. At another, she started acting more and more as if she were at home sharing a recipe with a friend, as when she told the audience, "Sorry, no dessert!" instead of stating as she had in earlier demonstrations, "We don't serve any dessert with this meal because it is already so rich."

Demonstrators also found that when they needed a break from people, they could retreat into the activity itself, "ignore people and just work," as Steve Jayton put it. Even though this refocusing of energy was a welcome relief, their activity still counted as demonstration (i.e., what they were supposed to be doing) since they were still on view. Bob

Jameson, Karl Arnold, Steve Jayton, and Will Davis were all amazed at the tenacity of watchers. Jameson described the attentiveness of the audience as "almost startling," far more intense than he had experienced with tourists who see his demonstrations in the Wooden Shoe factory in Holland, Michigan. Arnold described some of his audience as "practically taking out an apprenticeship" and regretted the lack of chairs for them. Apprenticeship, of course, is a learning mode, with the potential to key an instructional framing of the situation in the demonstrator.

Demonstration is, in its essence, always a secondary frame, "laminated" on top of a primary activity, and thus it co-exists fairly easily with most other interpretations. Note, for example, that Bob Jameson, who demonstrates the making of wooden shoes as his regular job, was engaged in a demonstration of a demonstration at the FAF (fascinating to us, unproblematic to him). Still, given that there is often more than one way to construe one's activity at the FAF, conflicts do arise. Steve Jayton generally adapted quite well to the festival environment, especially after he had rearranged his work area to make himself more comfortable. Nevertheless, he could never quite make the demonstration and work frames mesh in terms of proper clothing. He had brought along the clothes that he really uses at home for working on the boat, but was reluctant to be seen in them on the Mall. As a demonstrator he was also a representative of Michigan and a person making a first impression on the public. So his work clothes stayed wadded up in a corner of the hotel room while his good sport clothes got messy from being worked in.

Frame confusions caused particular difficulties for some participants. For Dave Ray and Gary Richards the whole festive/festival frame remained tenuous and problematic (on which see more below). Their participation in the FAF made most sense to them as just another one of the odd jobs with which both now support themselves. (The main kind of fishing they once practiced—gill-netting—is now banned in their area.) They consequently had less access from the beginning to the semiplay frame that makes re-enacting or objectifying one's own activity and experience easier. In addition, the kind of activity they were supposed to be demonstrating was more difficult to adapt than most because it involved whole body movement and required large movement through space (unlike cooking, woodworking, and sewing) and because its stage context (Mall) was much more different from its usual context (Great

g. 8   Gill-netting demonstration area   *Photo: Richard Anderson*

kes) than was the case for the demonstration kitchens and workshops
r smaller scale activities. As a result, the demonstration itself had to be
uch more like a dramatized enactment, even though: 1) these two men
re less prepared than most for "play-acting" because of their "work"
indset, 2) the scale of movement made voices almost impossible to
nplify adequately, and 3) the site, though planned to be a visual draw,
d not lend itself to dramatized demonstration (see above, Ralston's
gret that the site did not include a pond so that the nets could be
orked).* Ray and Richards soon recognized that by standing around
d talking to interested people who asked questions they were doing
at could be done with a large and somewhat inconvenient site. They

The staff had chosen the boat as one of the big visual draws they needed at the
tival, and talked about the site design like a stage set, a well-designed visual
ckdrop. The boat drew an audience all right, but when it got there, there was
leed nothing happening—no moving parts, no demonstrations involving
ving parts, and 'keep off, don't touch' signs.... Occupational settings are more
stly and time-consuming to prepare, and the Smithsonian staff has not been
paring and improving them with as much devotion and for as long as it has
sical, and perhaps craft and food, performance" (Gilmore 4-27-89, pp. 9–10).

consequently redefined their site as "a show place, not a talk place." Fellow fishermen Will Ralston and Neil Charles approached the situation differently when they arrived in the second week. Their technique was, in effect, to split frames apart, setting up the net over the boat as a pure display that could more easily speak for itself (although they felt that a more comprehensive photo display was required to tell the story fully) and then devoting their energies toward talking individually to visitors, using the site less as a stage than as a backdrop and reference point.

For participants on the demonstration stages, demonstration and performance flowed together fairly easily. Performance groups on the main stage, however, sometimes had to do some crucial negotiating for themselves. Presenters, by their very presence, framed the activity as demonstration, but they did not always intervene again to offer interpretation or explanation.

The Nowickis, who have plenty of energy, tremendous confidence in themselves and in the appeal of their music, and a designated (also voluble and creative) M.C., worked well and actively with their presenter, Jim Leary, and found little difficulty in adapting to and making use of this mixed performance-demonstration format. Our initial impression, derived only from observing their performances at the festival, was simply that the Nowickis were relatively sophisticated in their reflexive understanding of their own work and were improvising successful adaptations on that basis. Jim Nowicki (a salesman in everyday life and, in Jim Leary's phrase, an "entrepreneurial bandleader") easily slid back and forth between the role of hearty polka-band M.C. and demonstration explainer in a manner facilitated by his usual self-parodying style. (He never managed to comment on his own quite traditional talk style, however.) For the most part the Nowickis just performed, riding on the force of their music. But if it seemed that audience interest was lagging, they shifted into demonstration format, taking a reflexive step back to talk about some aspect of the tradition and their relation to it—essentially re-framing their performance as a re-creation or re-presentation of a polka fest performance. They told the audience enough about the fun-time settings in which they usually play to bring that context along with them and give this audience a taste of what it would be like to be there. Their discussion and demonstration of the three different kinds of polka music and the dance style that goes with each one did double duty in also demonstrating their sophistication and intellectual command of the tradition.

As Leary explained to us subsequently, however, he worked actively with the Nowickis to make them aware of their resources and to enable them to incorporate presenter functions into their stage activities with good effect:

> We had a lengthy discussion prior to their first appearance about the kind of audience they would play for, about the ignorance (and even aversion) of some of the OFP staff and the sound crew regarding polka music, about strategies for performance/demonstration/recontextualization (including highlighting "eastern," "honky," and "push" Polish styles and their accompanying dances), and about the importance of calling periodic attention to what they usually did when playing for their usual audiences. (Leary, correspondence, 7-4-88, p. 2)

The Simons, in contrast, had considerable difficulty finding a comfortable balance between performance and demonstration. It appears in retrospect (see also the example in section 4.0, below) that they may have begun to understand the fundamental demonstration aspect of the

Fig. 9   Balancing performance and demonstration frames   *Photo: Patricia Sawin*

festival (and, consequently, their role in exemplifying the variety of Michigan cultures and the transplantation of Southern culture to Michigan by migrants) only afterwards. Conceptualizing themselves as performers, albeit ones who perform largely for their own enjoyment and usually at small festivals where most groups are at about their skill level, the Simons were puzzled about their invitation to the Mall: "It's not because we're all that good, that's for sure,"* Mike Simon told Garry Barrow. Consequently they seemed a little insecure about their ability to meet the standards they believed were expected.

Having worked themselves up psychologically to perform in such a prestigious venue, the Simons then felt confused and undermined by accommodations on the Mall and the performance schedule. Lacking a green room for pre-performance preparations, they felt that they never did their best because by the time they actually got warmed up and in sync with each other they were almost through with the first set, and then, as they phrased it "there was no second set." They also noted that their one performance on the North Carolina stage occurred while the Nowickis were playing on the Michigan stage. Since the two main stages were placed directly across the Mall from each other and the polka music was so loud that the Simons could not hear their own monitors at all, they couldn't stay on key or in rhythm.

The issue of appropriate repertoire, however, caused the Simons the most difficulty and clearly revealed the struggles they were having in establishing a consistent and sustainable frame for their activities. In their interviews with Nick Spitzer before the festival, the Simons described their own aesthetic as preserving "Old-time country before country went pop" and expressed their interest in bringing out the deep roots of their tradition. They concluded, therefore, that they would not bring the banjo player whom they usually recruit when they are going to play for an audience expecting some Bluegrass tunes. In their first interview with Barrow at very beginning of the festival, they described themselves as in ideological step with the Smithsonian's perceived preservationist agenda: Mike said, "Our kind of music's dying out and

---

* Nick Spitzer offers an alternate interpretation. In his view, this statement is partly ironic, consistent with an Anglo self-effacing style regarding musical prowess. He adds that the Simons were chosen to represent Old-time, but not inferior style, to represent Anglo-Southern migration to the North, and to represent a family style.

probably will die out eventually. I think it's good that the Smithsonian is giving exposure of this kind of music to a wider audience."

But, although they had practiced some older songs prior to the festival and had sent a tape to Spitzer that included American ballads and sentimental parlor songs, they ultimately performed very few of these at the festival. These were songs that they remembered from their youth or perhaps used to sing together for fun, but rarely if ever performed, and which seemed (whether from the performers' rustiness or the audience's lack of familiarity) to have less obvious appeal (see section 2.3 for a discussion of the possible influence of Barrow's intervention). The Simons were not themselves prepared to supply the kind of contextualization that these pieces would probably have needed to go over well, and their presenter, Nick Spitzer, elected not to intervene to provide song-by-song commentary.* Left on their own, the Simons framed their activity as an instance of what they knew best—performance,** not demonstration. They valued audience reception more than the more abstract goal of taking the opportunity to promote older songs. In so doing they largely related to the FAF audience as if its needs and expectations were the same as those of an ordinary bluegrass festival audience and, in Mike's words, ended up "just doing what we always did."[14]

Finally, the Yemeni performance group exemplified how difficult it is to transform what is usually a participation event into an interesting yet "natural looking" performance. They characterized the dances they do as "village dances," and it appeared that the group itself had worked out some minimal choreographies so as to transform dances they occasionally engage in at private celebrations in their expatriate community in Detroit into an ethnic symbol and display form for outsiders. They had developed a dance demonstration that worked fairly well at small-scale Arab community or city-wide festivals in Detroit. It made only brief attempts to sustain a full performance frame and was amplified with

---

* Spitzer felt the Simonses "were overzealously caught up in their own antiquarian sense of cultural revival," and that they didn't perform the ballads and other material as well. He felt "they would do better with their usual repertoire which, in fact, was marked as 'Old-time' more by style [a fiddle-driven, old-time sound] than repertoire" (personal communication).

** Nick Spitzer notes that the talk stages he conducted with the Simonses were planned as demonstration and discussed as such with them beforehand. These demonstrations effectively made the point that their music was a response to the migration experience.

audience participation and a "fashion show." The costume display was ruled out for FAF performances, however, since Anglo women do the costume modeling in these public displays (because it is considered improper for Yemeni women to do so). The Yemenis were also handicapped by having a new group of dancers who were not quite prepared, technically or psychologically. Having their activities framed as full performance on the big stage only exacerbated the problem. The dancers attempted to return to a participatory event by coming down off the stage and having audience members dance with them, although in so doing they retreated from an accurate re-presentation of Yemeni culture, since men and women do not touch or dance together traditionally in these dances.*

The differences among the Simons, the Nowickis, and the Yemeni dancers in terms of their experience of and ability to adapt to performance on an FAF "main stage" are doubtless traceable to a variety of factors (including personality and individual agendas) not controllable by festival staff. The comparison of these three instances (and between this group and the two immediately preceding examples) strongly suggests, however, that a touch of the demonstration frame in what is other-wise framed as performance is more difficult and less intuitive for participants than the reverse process.

3.4.2 Previous Recontextualizing Experience. We anticipated that people who had previous experience in framing or re-presenting the activity in which they were involved at the FAF would have an easier time adapting to the festival frame. This proved true, but we found that what counted as "recontextualizing experience" was quite variable and subtle. Involvement

---

* "The problems of the Yemeni performance in an audience setting reinforce the point about having groups without sufficient advance discussion or rationale other than filling in ethnic representation (a problem found especially in the Michigan sociopolitical landscape). On the other hand, the Cultural Conservation of Language program across the Mall had a very different model. There the traditional and changing community dance forms of southeast Asian refugee groups were presented with efforts to get local community network members out to the event. The result was a group's ability to truly take over and recontextualize themselves with weight of numbers of understanding people in the audience. The general audience member then didn't have to see an entertaining performance as much as witness an emergent recontextualization made even more exciting by its location on the Mall at FAF" (Nick Spitzer, personal communication).

in another "festival" was helpful only to the extent that the FAF was actually like the previously-experienced festival, allowing the participant to sustain familiar definitions. Although Raymond Leslie was initially disappointed with the mild audience response at the FAF, where he was less flashy than some other performers, his extensive experience in playing at Old Time Fiddlers' jamborees ultimately seemed to stand him in good stead. Spending days performing, jamming, and hobnobbing with other musicians was already part of his life (cf. Spitzer 1987:9) and he found ways to be comfortable in those familiar activities with other musicians while he got his bearings. The Nowickis, similarly, especially after their coaching from Jim Leary, were able to draw upon their experience at polka festivals (and to reflect on the significance of their various performance contexts) to adapt well on stage either to do a straight performance or to re-frame performance as a demonstration. For the Simons, in contrast, their experience at bluegrass festivals was actually deleterious, because it provided them a model that seemed reliable, but was not quite appropriate for the FAF, raising their anxiety and steering them away from the repertoire they had originally intended to present. For Bob Jameson, his extensive practical experience with doing demonstrations at work and with arranging "remotes" for trade shows and nearby festivals made his FAF experience very simple and painless, but perhaps thus also denied him the full advantage of the recontextualizing experience. The FAF was not nearly as special to him as to most other participants—just another day at work.

Other kinds of (non-festival) experience turned out to be just as, if not more helpful, though not necessarily in predictable ways. Previous experience with a festival (in Michigan) did not provide Steve Jayton and Will Davis much guidance because it was so unlike the FAF and led them to expect quite a different physical set-up and audience. What they did find, however, was that their experience as river guides proved to be an important ongoing resource for them in adapting to the FAF. As they explained it, at one and the same time, guiding is practical activity, demonstration/instruction, and performance (of expert fishing or graceful propulsion of the boat) and requires the guide to become a "diplomat for a day," learning how to interact at close quarters with clients who exhibit a wide variety of personality types. The skills they have developed over the years in guiding thus proved applicable as they responded to repetitive questions, got used to being watched while they worked, and so on. Hope Miller Lawson, a high school English teacher who participated in the North Carolina segment of the Language Conservation program, was another example of someone whose professional skills (in this case, both speaking in front of large audiences and having previously developed an ideology about the importance of valuing Appalachian dialect) meshed with what the festival required of her. Lawson's communication skills and her well-developed ability to get people to join an activity also had a significant influence on bringing members of different ethnic groups together during the evening parties.

Practical, logistical aspects of the activity to be represented also determined the extent to which participants could find useful models in their prior experience. Those people who were involved in fairly small-scale activities (cooking, embroidery, egg decorating, fly-tying, even wood working and boat building), which in their usual context are taught by showing accompanied by explaining, generally adapted easily to festival presentations. They already had experience (albeit essentially unrecognized as such) doing a form of demonstration. The participant's intellectual conception of his/her activity was important as well, however. Those who already saw their activity as slightly set aside from the everyday, as art or the maintenance of tradition or an essential part of an ethnic identity, had already performed one of the most crucial adjustments. Those, in contrast, who regarded what they were doing as simply their occupation had a much larger transition to make in order to understand how they could qualify as folk and their activity as folklife. Indeed, participants at times disputed the labels ascribed to them, as we will explore in the next section.

3.4.3 Negotiation/Resistance/Survival. For the most part, participants enjoyed their involvement in the festival: they received various benefits that made up for the stresses endured and they got increasingly caught up in the festival spirit. However, they did not always agree with or appreciate the identities they felt were being ascribed to them. While carrying out their duties responsibly on-stage, backstage they found various ways (often creative and humorous) to re-negotiate identity, offer resistance, or simply to survive the two weeks. This reflexive process was accomplished during informal conversations and off hours, such as during meals or bus trips from the hotel to the Mall. This talk also revealed that, in their efforts to figure out their own roles and the standards of behavior expected/allowed at the FAF, participants continually evaluated other participants in comparison to themselves.

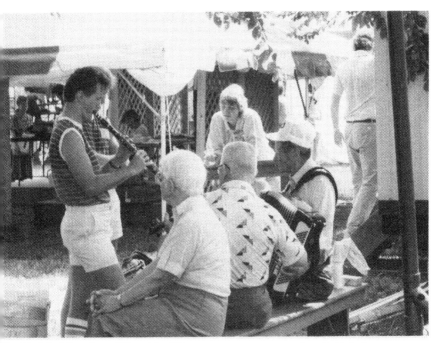

Fig. 10   Musicians from different traditions

Photo: Patricia Sawin

Fig. 11   Jamming at the North Carolina area of the Language Conservation Program

Photo: Richard Bauman

Several of the people involved in the FAF in 1987 did not perceive themselves as involved in a folk activity by any stretch of the imagination. Lewis VanBuskirk, a master carver for a major manufacturer of expensive period reproduction wood furniture, justified his presence at the FAF as akin to his participation in crafts shows, and used demonstrations to emphasize process and technique. On a visit to the Cultural Conservation section, he took the opportunity to scatter his business cards around the work area of traditional Mexican-American carver Sandor Chavez, thereby publicizing his company and apparently establishing a distance between his own identity and that of a "folk carver."

Davis and Jayton were acutely conscious and proud of the fact that river guiding was a tradition in their families and that this "pedigree" was probably why they in particular had been chosen for the FAF. Davis revealed something of his self-image when he suggested that Crocodile Dundee was a favorite movie and that he, like its lead character, "also creates the impression of great knowledge out of simple common sense." For example, Davis knows particular places along the river where fish always strike and he tells his city-folk clients to cast there. They get a bite every time and are duly impressed by his river-guiding expertise. But both Davis and Jayton rejected what Davis labeled the "folksy" subtext of "folklife." Before coming to the festival, Davis had worried about being treated as a backwoods hick by the audiences in D.C., but at the end of the two weeks he remarked, "If anybody treated me that way, it was someone from the Smithsonian, it wasn't the people."

Talk stages made many of the participants feel uncomfortable and objectified. "Must be fifty people there before we start, but they all leave when we come on," laughed Will Davis. Presenters essentially could ask anything, although in most cases they took the opportunity to discuss admissible topics with participants in advance. Will Davis and Steve Jayton disliked "spilling their guts on stage," though they reluctantly complied. All made discretionary choices among various perceived options. For example, participants drew a line between private and public narratives, protecting their private selves from public scrutiny by refusing to yield to on-stage prodding to tell narratives they had shared freely during friendly, informal interaction with presenters. Gary Richards had considerable difficulty with the "Comparative Fish Stories" sessions (especially the first one) because he defined himself as an occupational fisherman in contrast to the sports fishermen with whom neither he nor

Fig. 12 "Becoming a diplomat" for the day   *Photo: Richard Bauman*

Fig. 13 Fishermen interacting on the talk stage   *Photo: Patricia Sawin*

his presenter anticipated that he would be paired. Sports fishermen had traditional "lies" to tell, while he was telling personal and "true" narratives about serious and in some instances painful experiences, which he felt might have seemed maudlin or even slightly ridiculous among all the whopper tall tales. Dave Ray, who maintained that participating in the talk stage had not been part of his contract, simply balked and refused to take part at all. Meshin, the leader of the Yemeni group, directly contradicted his presenter's on-stage assertion that most of the people who had migrated to Michigan were from the working classes. But this kind of baldly serious refusal to play along was atypical.

Most of the negotiation was playful. Will Davis, for example, enjoyed turning the tables on the presenters, "getting them to answer my questions, for a change," or usurping the presenter's role by posing his own questions to his co-participants. Davis seemed to be calling for on-stage equality between participant/presenter: he too had knowledgeable and appropriate questions to ask. (By taking the lead, Davis [and similarly other participants] exercised one of the options that Nick Spitzer identifies as developing in the interviewer/interviewee context, i.e., participants turn the tables and use their speaking abilities to show their competence as tradition-bearers and to foreground the importance and validity of their efforts). But while Spitzer envisions a collaboration in which "much complex role playing can be done as people may choose to be portrayed as the unmitigated purveyors by the 'pro' who validates them" and as participants who "are quite comfortable with the interview initially, become more independent as the days go by" (Nick Spitzer, personal communication), the participants with whom we worked talked much more about the power conferred on the presenter in his/her sanctioned role as interrogator (see, e.g., Goody 1978; Samarin 1967:144–45).

Phil Stephens, representing Michigan cherry growers, tended to disassociate himself entirely from the notion of folklife. Stephens serves as the agricultural extension agent for his area, and as he saw it, he had been invited only because the people who do treat the skills of tree care as a sort of customary wisdom were all too busy making their living at cherry harvests at the time of the festival. On one occasion, he was urged by a presenter to include more folklife in his presentation. By his account, he did not respond directly at the time, but when reporting the incident over supper (a setting in which talk often served as psychological sustenance), he capped his recounting of the encounter with the exclamation, "Folklife? What do I know about folklife?" and received appreciative laughter from Davis, Jayton, and Jameson.

This narrative launched a series of fantasies about jokes participants could carry out at (and about) the festival, such as ways to take control by creating chaos on the last day by exchanging booths, or gluing a quarter to the bow of a boat and watching passers-by try to pick it up. In the course of accumulating experiences and interactions, and as strangers became acquaintances and even friends, sociability intensified and talk, parody, and laughter about their circumstances and about the events of each day proved therapeutic. Rose Jenner's anecdote about accidentally locking one of the staff members in the Jiffy John and saying to him when he finally emerged, "I didn't recognize you without your pants down," was greeted with humorous appreciation for this concrete breaking of hierarchical boundaries. Stephens teased Jameson in a way that revealed his sympathetic understanding that carving wooden shoes at the Festival had come to limit and define Jameson in uncomfortable but also funny ways, while the Leslies good-naturedly "heckled" (their word) Jameson from the audience. Stephens and Jameson later collaborated on a song about the prominently labelled "Zoo Bus" (presumably borrowed from the Washington Zoo and used to transport participants from the hotel to the Mall), suggesting, in joking fashion, that the name accurately reflected their feeling of being treated at times more like creatures on display than as people.

Behind-the-scenes humor enabled participants to renew their own self-definitions while maintaining an acceptable performance persona. Phil Stephens' oft-repeated story about a woman who looked at the cherry pitter and asked, "Does this machine make cherries?" depicted the questioner as stupid, allowing the participant to laugh at her instead of being annoyed, and at the same time to reassert and enjoy his own expertise. When audiences were especially rude or patronizing, however, participants sometimes also found what they hoped were humorous but effective ways to throw the intended stereotype back in their faces. Rose Jenner described one such situation during a North Carolina foodways demonstration:

> Mary Greene was our presenter. And she'd go and tell like: I'm a nurse and I work forty hours a week and I sing ballads and I probably don't cook as much as my grandmother did. She'd go into detail about me and my

grandmother. And one of the ladies from the audience spoke up and she said, "I have a question for Rose," and she looked at me and she said, [new voice tone, condescending] "Rose, since you hold down a full-time job and you've got a husband, do you own a microwave?" I just looked at her and laughed. I thought, "God." I said, "Yes ma'am." ["ma'am" very drawn out] I kind of did it on purpose to play on the Southern accent. I just wanted to say, "Yes, and I have a dishwasher and I've got a washer and drier, refrigerator." Because it just flipped me out that she didn't think that we would own microwaves down here in the South.

Most festival participants pride themselves on being "traditional," either by continuing a family occupation, talent, or practice, or by learning one that is personally significant. They do, then, use the term "folk" self-referentially. Among the FAF participants, however, were those who seemed particularly sensitive to and offended by being perceived or treated as "folksy," in the sense of unsophisticated, untravelled, uneducated people without political views and agendas. One young participant, for example, resisted what he described as the patronizing tone of FAF staff when he tried to convey to them that he regarded himself as a seasoned international traveler who could handle the logistics of getting his display to D.C. He noted that in pre-festival phone conversations, he gradually (but painfully) developed a good working understanding with his staff contact. He was stunned, therefore, when he met this person face-to-face in D.C. and was treated—once more— like "an absolute mental cretin that didn't know what was going on." Festival staff have to accommodate a wide range of participants, from rural seniors to urban elites. At the 1987 festival, it was clear that FAF staff and their field consultants seek to include participants who stretch popular conceptions of what "folk" and "folklore" encompass. Yet perceptions by participants of an undifferentiated treatment not only undermine such impulses, but perhaps also suggest that models seem currently to have outpaced practices.

In addition to relations with staff and audiences at a "folklife festival," the situation of being studied by "folklorists" (at that moment, the IU team) also involves an implicit ascription of the "folk" label as well as issues of hierarchy and permission to interrogate, so it is not surprising that participants played with the researchers in resistance-based ways. Louis Kettunen developed one of the most elaborately reflexive responses to the uncomfortable situation of being studied by folklorists. Kettunen is a social worker, his wife teaches Finnish, and he is both dedicated to performing Finnish music and highly conscious of the ironies involved in putting on folksy costumes and playing an ethnic part. His response was to involve the audience in a joke at the expense of the folklorists. During a performance one of the members of the group stumbled over the words in a song in Finnish and then stopped singing for a couple of lines while getting his bearings again. Kettunen first explained, though no one in the audience was taken in, that it was an old Finnish custom to leave out the words to particularly racy parts of songs. Then he looked straight at Richard Bauman and commented, "I've got to stop lying to these folklorists!" as if to say to the audience, "We all know that we're here just to have a good time, only the egg heads are trying to interpret it and get all kinds of deep meaning." For the objectified subject, telling a joke with a straight face and having it taken for truth is a form of power that throws a monkey wrench in the scholarly works (see Paredes 1977). Kettunen used the technique adroitly, but with a further twist, since he knew that Bauman knew precisely what he was doing, in effect, taking a stab at the folklorists and simultaneously establishing himself as an intellectual able to play the reflexive games. Although none of us worked in depth with Kettunen, his reaction could easily have been more widely applicable.

As noted above, many of the participants were impressed with the tenacity of people who came to watch them and they tried to devise creative means to encourage and facilitate prolonged attention. At the same time, however, practically everyone who did continuous demonstrations (musical performers and people in foodways who only did one or two shows a day seemed relatively immune) soon grew bored with repeating themselves and answering the same questions, which grew to appear increasingly inane. Few seem to have anticipated this part of the festival experience. Those with past festival experience described audiences who were knowledgeable about local traditions and therefore asked fewer questions. Participants' responses to repetitious questions demonstrate the ways in which they were continually testing the bounds of the possible in the festival realm, weighing their own needs against what they thought was expected of them.

Ray and Richards wistfully expressed a desire to make a tape that would "answer the same stupid questions" over and over again, but they actually adapted by doing more demonstrations. Arnold and Davis contented themselves by simply describing in conversations with sympathetic fellow participants the outrageous responses they would have *liked* to have given to audiences. Arnold threatened that if one more person asked him, "What are you doing?" as he sat embroidering, he was going to respond, "Painting my toe nails!" Davis often doubted that people listened to his answers to their routine questions and reported being sorely tempted to start his response by telling them he was "the son of a Polish immigrant from Vietnam" just to test them (an answer also adapted from his river-guiding). At the same time, Davis had little respect for participants with memorized, pat responses ("salesmen's raps") who did not appropriately fulfill his idea of what festival participants should do.

About three days into the festival, Bob Jameson put sentiment into action by posting a sign: "The wood I use is aspen." He recognized that the implied "stupid" question was also the easiest opening for someone who wanted to initiate a conversation and while he regretted stifling audience-participant interaction, he left the sign up because he couldn't stand the repetition. Davis and Jayton, who had bonded closely with the volunteer in their tent, taught him the basic questions and answers. He greeted the public—becoming a kind of human-equivalent to Jameson's sign—while they were left free to work on the boat.

Semi-serious, resistance-based joking allowed participants and presenters alike to play with the boundaries, to adjust their self-images before a sympathetic group of fellow-participants, and to assert the higher value of defining everyone there as people who enjoy and value tradition, regardless of the dichotomizing and hierarchial tendency of the routine festival day. A demonstration of such idealized leveling developed in the North Carolina section of Cultural Conservation, where several of us spent some time. On an afternoon when none of the North Carolina musicians was performing on the main stage, presenter Glenn Hinson gathered his group in the mock tobacco barn and orchestrated a "kitchen-picking" session during which, in addition to the full complement of musicians from North Carolina, Hinson himself was playing spoons and Richard Bauman was playing guitar (Hinson introduced Bauman simply as "our friend," saying nothing about his being a folklorist). Mike Simon was making a video-tape for his own use and Marion Simon was holding a tape recorder for another of the Indiana ethnographers, who was busily singing along.

14   A "kitchen-picking" session   *Photo: Richard Bauman*

3.4.4 Definitional Conflicts. In addition to figuring out how to define
~~r~~ own activities at the festival, participants must engage with and are
~~s~~equently affected by other definitions, namely, those of presenters,
~~cu~~torial staff, or production staff. When interacting with the production
~~staff,~~ participants are asked to experience the festival principally as a show
~~sp~~ectacle. The success of the show (and the value of the producers) is
~~dete~~rmined by audience reaction and by the smoothness of the presenta-
~~tion~~ from an audience standpoint (e.g., technical quality of sound produc-
~~tion,~~ no gaps in the program).

~~   P~~articipants also experienced differences (sometimes consciously ac-
~~kno~~wledged, sometimes not) with presenters, curatorial staff, or others
~~who~~ assumed responsibility for the message to be conveyed by particular
~~even~~ts. When presenters and participants already knew each other well,
~~they~~ also tended to agree on the interpretations that should be presented
~~and~~ were able to work as a team. But in other instances, participants had a
~~diffe~~rent sense of what could be learned from such an event, framed it

differently, or found themselves in direct, conscious disagreement with staff. These problems most often cropped up if they were working with a relative stranger as presenter or if they did not find out about an activity until the show was underway—which meant they could not "escape"—or if they felt that a private self was being put at risk in public.

Comparative talk sessions seemed particularly acute settings for these types of problems to appear. In the instance of the commercial and recreational fishermen (see above, section 3.4.3), the exchange among the two groups was apparently intended to represent both, showing that they use the same resources in different ways, with different philosophies. Given the sharp differences felt by the participating individuals, however, it was difficult for participants to background their immediate personal reactions and adapt to the more abstract educational goals of the session.[15]

Some problems cannot be anticipated (clashes over the need for practice time as opposed to the need for quiet on the bus, for example), others have become an expected part of the FAF (the competitiveness between groups over control of the floor at the evening parties). Some conflicts, however, seem to be built into the discipline and the choice of participants. The traditions folklorists recognize as worthy of study are often threatened or marginal; they are the old ways that may be in conflict with "enlightened" new policies, so politics and strong convictions are involved. Folklorists are increasingly aware of such issues and are interested in communicating them in the festival format. But participants can be expected to act on and to interpret the festival in terms of their own prior or intuitive frames and agendas rather than the frame and agendas of festival planners, unless they have the opportunity to engage actively in preparatory discussion of the (often sensitive) political dimensions of festival representations as well as the kinds of reframing (of conflicts into issues) involved especially in educational, comparative programming.

3.4.5 *Reputation*. To conclude our consideration of participants' "framing" of their festival activity, it is essential to emphasize that whether performing or demonstrating, participants felt they were putting their reputations on the line. Several remarked that they were not consulted beforehand about what to expect, what to bring, or how their space would (or could) be designed to make it easier to work in and hence to produce more effective performances. Those who were happiest were those who either brought their own portable work environment (Bob Jameson) or were free to rearrange their area to suit themselves (Steve Jayton). Those who were unhappiest were those (like the Great Lakes fishermen) who had to accept a physical layout that because of its massive scale could be little altered on-site. Several participants specifically noted that they could have and would have liked to have helped put their displays together.

In smaller and more immediate matters, both staff and participants are embarrassed when signals are crossed, but it is often the participant who must take responsibility before the audience: Steve Jayton who loses his concentration when he can't make fish and pancakes come off the grill at the same time (the customary pairing on his camp menu) because the fish supplied is five times the size of his usual brook trout; Phil Stephens who looks the fool when he tries to tell people that cherry pitting machines do a good, neat job, while the demonstration machine he must use has sour-cherry cups and is turning the large sweet cherries he must work with into mush. In other words, even those who are basically doing demonstrations find that being on display evokes a performative reaction. They personally want to do well and look good.

In general, participants tend to take their own activity fairly seriously. The prior commitment common among those skilled enough to have been chosen as cultural representatives is reinforced by their awareness of being paid by the Smithsonian for their performances. Thus, they are disconcerted when they encounter what they perceive as unprofessionalism, or when they must act within seeming chaos: "fifteen different people doing fifteen different things and hoping and praying the damn thing works," as one participant observed.

Because the lack of materials can potentially cause the person on stage considerable embarrassment, it was frequently mentioned by participants (although at times half jokingly, as with the lack of rutabagas for pasties, or the need to debone a chicken on stage with a fork).[16] On the up side, participants were quick to notice and appreciate the staff's resourcefulness in performing seeming miracles of procurement, as in the case of tracking down extra muskrat from one of the Arabbers on the other side of the Mall.

Several participants report slowly realizing a pressure to display multiple talents. From their point of view, there were two interrelated difficulties inherent in being asked to perform in multiple roles. Those who interpreted their festival involvement as a species of work or who were losing money by coming to D.C. took their contracts very seriously. Consequently, they were aware that some of the sessions for which they were scheduled on the program (prominently, the talk stage) as well as many of the activities that evolved in the second week were not explicitly figured into the way they were being paid. Second, participants' egos and reputations were on the line in these secondary presentations just as much as in their main assignments, and they often felt it was hard for them to do a respectable job without adequate preparation or access to tools and materials that they could have brought from home if asked beforehand.* A certain territoriality tends to develop between practitioners of the same art, and thus when participants are asked to share space and resources, they may feel both uncomfortable and frustrated at being prevented from displaying their skills to best advantage. In several instances, the Smithsonian sought to present diversity within a tradition, yet in the process sometimes overlooked the personal needs of the people who practice diverse styles. When Will Davis was asked to tie flies in Sue Rodnitzky's space, he likened it to "being in the ladies' locker room." As quickly as possible, he set up his own demonstration space in the boatbuilding area he shared with Steve Jayton, but the resulting distance from Rodnitzky's area hampered ready comparison of techniques. Will Ralston, it will be remembered, was incredulous at the suggestion that he help smoke fish in a refrigerator (see section 3.0). It appears that a contradiction, probably inadvertent, is operating here. The participants' resourcefulness and creativity, especially in being able to recast any activity into a presentation form, seems highly valued by the festival staff. Yet, without warning beforehand about the variety of skills they might be asked to demonstrate and the preparations they might need to make, the participants cannot fully take control of recontextualizing their activities once they are on-site at the Mall.

* The presenter/fieldworkers' credibility was also at stake in these situations: One presenter said if he had known that language conservation was a significant topic, he could have chosen a different foodways representative, less accomplished at cooking, but much more involved in the language and hence probably a better representative of the culture overall.

4.0 After-effects and Recollections in Tranquility

For the most part, when interviewed three to eight weeks after the end of the Festival of American Folklife, participants demonstrated positive attitudes toward the experience. With the passing of time, any perceived slights and infelicities encountered in D.C. had faded. Even the Simons, who never managed to play a set they were really proud of in D.C., said they would do it again if given the chance. Several participants spoke enthusiastically of benefits expected or received. Karl Arnold had been sure that recognition by the Smithsonian would "trigger research sources" and he had subsequently been proved correct. Polly Elder talked a lot about the education she had received by meeting so many different people (quite a wonderful experience for a seventy-year-old who had wanted to be a teacher, but never got the chance to go past high school) and about the new friends from all over Michigan whom they planned to visit in the fall. Ray Leslie was less vocal, but gave evidence of having gained a certain increased confidence in himself.

The benefits of the festival spread beyond immediate participants, for example to two friends of the Elders (pictured in the festival handbook) who are also centrally engaged in the muskrat cooking, but were too sick and frail to consider a trip to D.C. They received vicarious enjoyment of this validation of their tradition, and the Elders felt good about being able to make these friends happy. Bob Jameson benefitted from the festival in a fashion not anticipated by usual models of "the folk." Stories abound regarding traditional craftspeople who get so many orders or such publicity from being in a festival that they are able to buy a new house, bring in running water, or implement some equally major lifestyle change. Jameson's personal economic situation did not change as a result of his participation in the FAF. The Wooden Shoe Factory in Holland, Michigan, however, was still receiving an increased volume of orders in late August as a result of exposure produced by Jameson's involvement in the FAF, and Jameson (who holds a degree in marketing and works in that capacity as well as a crafts demonstrator) was receiving recognition for his business acumen.

Not surprisingly, the prestige of being invited to the festival can cause friction between those who go and those involved in the same tradition who were not asked to participate or who for whatever reasons cannot accept the invitation. One festival musician had a falling out with a fellow-fiddler friend who initially had been invited but could not go to the festival. By the time he was reinterviewed in August, the two had put the bad feelings behind them. The Elders encountered both hometown jealousy and minor celebrity. Some of the people who belong to the club where they serve muskrat dinners treated them rather coldly, while complete strangers would come up to them in the shopping mall to say, "It couldn't happen to a nicer couple!" Whether this recognition will have any lasting impact on the popularity of the muskrat tradition remains to be seen, but it is worth noting that, in the interpretation of Dennis Au (curator at the local museum who served as the Elders' presenter at the FAF), people in Monroe, Michigan, were eager to make a fuss over the Elders mostly because they would like to find a symbol for the town that would be a little more glamorous than the Lazy-Boy chair headquarters and a little less laughable than being General Custer's hometown.

As was the case with many other aspects of the festival, those called upon to folklorize occupational pursuits had noticeably different experiences from the majority. Among one participant's family, what people seemed to remember about his participation was that they were, in their interpretation, "lied to" about the size of the sign they were promised to thank a cousin for donating the demonstration nets. (They evidently took descriptions of the approximately 4' by 8' photo and text display signs on which they *were* listed along with other contributors to mean that an entire sign that size would be devoted to acknowledging and publicizing their contribution.) In Will Ralston's hometown hardly anyone knows they went to Washington, and, although they had a good time (except for being rather overwhelmed by the number of people), they remain uncertain why they were even asked to go. Among the participants with whom we worked, however, these were the exception. The others sometimes offered constructive criticisms, but basically looked back on the FAF as a memorable and worthwhile experience.

5.0 Reprise: The Festival of Michigan Folklife

Most participants found their involvement in the Michigan-only festival at East Lansing in August easier and more relaxed than the first-time-through event in D.C. Instead of being faced with a strange new experience, participants felt involved in a reunion of old friends—a "family reunion," Marion Simon called it—on-stage and off. Those involved in comparative talk stages, for example Mike Simon and Ray Leslie, had gotten used to each other and were more relaxed and humorous and also (perhaps as a result of having had time to reflect on the matter) more able to articulate their philosophies vis-à-vis performance and festivals. Dennis Au, who had served as the Elders' presenter in D.C., was prevented by other responsibilities from participating in the Michigan festival, but Harry and Polly were sufficiently confident of their presentational abilities and sufficiently well-rehearsed in their demonstrations to manage fine without him. Janet Gilmore reports that she even convinced Gary Richards to try smoking some fish in this setting even though, like Ralston, he was "appalled and offended by the fish smoking apparatus present at the FAF site." Gilmore continues:

> Complaining all the way, Richards the perfectionist set to work, collaborating with other participants, volunteers, and myself to scrounge for proper parts and equipment, whip the refrigerator into shape, and smoke some fish. The whole business absorbed him well but made him very nervous, because he got a lot of attention and he sets great store on producing quality smoked fish using the right fish, right recipe, and right equipment (only the recipe was right). His reputation and ego were, as you put it, "on the line," and when he gave a comparative fish smoking presentation with . . . Chuck Cambry, whose ingredients differed, he felt threatened. But did he receive positive responses! He had an activity in which he could involve fellow participants like blacksmith Sanford Russet to express camaraderie and demonstrate their ingenuity and skill, he had a concrete topic (process and ingredients) about which he could talk at length with a very interested audience, and he produced a superb delight that brought him acclaim from fellow participants, presenters, and other staff. When asked about the incident, he still complains about the circum-

stances; but I think he enjoyed the attention and success, which boosted his ego at the time and later back home (Gilmore, 4-27-89, p. 6).

Those participants who had been disappointed in Washington because of all the additional information they would have brought, if only they'd known, could now compensate, thereby taking more control over the shape of their presentations. Many were also close enough to home to send someone to fetch additional materials that they decided they needed in the course of the festival.

The overall atmosphere was more informal, which also let people experiment with format, and, in particular, present "performances" more like those appropriate in their accustomed contexts. The Yemenis augmented their dancing and music with the "fashion show" they use at Detroit street festivals, with clothing modeled by two blonde American women. Rowena Leslie taught dances to children while her husband played.

The simpler organization of this smaller festival and the influence of organizers Marsha MacDowell and Kurt Dewhurst's greater in-depth knowledge and long-term acquaintance with a majority of participants also contributed to participants' positive experience. Our observations of this reprise of the Michigan section of the FAF emphasize the benefits of tapping into strong in-state programs, if it can be done without co-opting local folklorists' efforts. Indeed, were a local or state festival held *first*, so that the *FAF* would be the reunion, perhaps participants would feel more comfortable, sure of themselves, and in control.*

---

* Nick Spitzer adds, on the basis of his past experience, that he concurs about the advantages of the state festival having the curatorial control, in-depth knowledge, and reunion quality. In his view, one reason the 1985 Louisiana program was successful—termed 'the best state program we ever had at the festival' by the former OFP director—was because the majority of the participants had been together at local and state festivals. Six years of field survey had also acquainted many of the participants and presenters in advance. Although the Smithsonian funding fell into place only two and a half months before the event, the metacommunity of Louisiana program participants was much longer in the making (personal communication).

6.0   Conclusions

We have tried to share some of the richness and complexity of participants' experiences at the 1987 Festival of American Folklife as we observed and documented them. From the profusion of details two central observations emerge. First, it is clear that participants are extremely active. They are always thinking and acting: developing their performances day by day with or without staff requests for change, working to figure out just what they should and could be doing within the festival frame, constantly adapting, yet as quickly offering firm but usually good-humored resistance to definitions and demands at odds with their self-images, understandings, and goals. Participants, however, lack the prior experience that enables OFP staff and long-time presenters (who know that "things will come together" during the days of the festival) to accept chaos, uncertainty, and a degree of disorganization as part of the task at hand. Consequently, most participants cannot feel reassured that "things always work out" and that they are doing exactly their part by so actively meeting head-on the contingencies of festival participation.

Second, an adequate understanding of participant experience must recognize that, whether performing or demonstrating, people are putting their egos and reputations on the line every day in a variety of expected and unexpected formats. They take both their own activities and their obligations to the Smithsonian seriously and are constantly evaluating themselves and searching for standards of measurement from other participants' comments, from their own observations of other participants' activities, from perceived staff goals and attitudes (communicated directly or guessed at), and from audience reactions. Room for misevaluation and misconception at many and sometimes crucial points is great and can subsequently affect later activities, moods, and interactions.

A folklife festival, as we think our data concretely demonstrate, is a complex, dynamic, and highly problematic undertaking, in which a number of factors (themselves highly subject to revision in the course of the festival) intersect: personal agendas for participating, hierarchies of relating among disparate categories of individuals, and the need to draw upon, to adapt, and to reframe customary activities so as to make of them a representation intelligible to the festival audience and acceptable to folklorists and to the participants themselves.

APPENDIX I

The Festival of American Folklife Project: Research Guide

1. *Issues*

1.1 Festival organizers, public sector fieldworkers, and folklorists have debated the degree to which festivals realize their didactic and ideological objectives (*JEMF, Camp*).

1.2 Less discussed, but of even greater urgency are the issues concerning the impact that public sector folk festivals have—as events and as institutionalized cultural interventionalism—on the performers and craftspeople who participate (Carey, Mullen, Bauman), on the represented traditions and recreated performances (Cadaval, Bauman, Carey, Mullen), and on the groups and communities from which the participants are selected. In broad terms, these are the issues which this project seeks to address.

2. *Plan of Research*

2.1 Our focus on the performers' experience of participating in the Festival will be pursued in three phases, with points of interest specific to each phase:

a) before the festival, as the participants prepare themselves to go;

b) during the festival, as they accommodate to the festival context and engage in their presentational activities;

c) after the festival, as they look back on the experience and relate it to their subsequent practice of what they do.

2.2 Observation during the middle phase—during the festival—is central to our two primary concerns: a) the effects of participation on the enactment, re-creation, and/or performance of sociocultural behaviors in the festival context; b) the participants' actual experience of being in the festival.

2.3 We anticipate consequences of participation in this event on several levels, including:

a) performance/re-creation (artistic and communicative);

b) personal and pragmatic (benefits, aggravations, conveniences, compromises);

c) social (community attitudes toward participants, tradition, festival);

d) ideological (perception of self, tradition, government).

2.4 Researchers will cover each of the four usual components of the Festival: music, crafts, occupation, and foodways.

2.5 Our research will also take into account the following variables, and attempt to study people who represent both ends of each spectrum:

a) prior experience in presenting/displaying what they do—ranging from those who have been performers, even at festivals, craft fairs, etc., to those who have not before framed what they do as display;

b) range of public visibility in home community, before and after—especially relevant because of the Smithsonian's avowed intent to bring unknown folk artists to the attention of the local community;

c) gender and age: whether these have a regular, observable effect on partici-pants' adaptation to festival self-presentation, or whether other factors or indi-vidual personality traits make the difference;

d) dimensions of identity: whether the participant sees him/herself as an individual artist or as a representative of a social group;

e) whether the participant comes to the festival alone or is accompanied by familiar companions with whom s/he can discuss the experience and work out necessary personal and performative adaptations.

3. Theoretical perspective

3.1 Recent models of culture and society envision both as processual recreations of relations and meanings, and stress the centrality of agency and situatedness in these processes.

3.2 Specific traditional behaviors are deeply rooted in particular social contexts within which interactionally-sustained and defined frames, meanings, and ways of doing are available as resources for individuals to communicate, achieve ends, to renegotiate the means and meanings—available for the enactment, staging, and interpretation of expressive interactions and cultural events.

3.3 Folk festivals as such are peculiarly modern phenomena—"cultural produc-tions" (MacCannell) wherein behaviors which have their primary basis in the social life of particular communities are self-consciously presented/recreated (Schechner) for popular, touristic (MacCannell), and political (Whisnant) constitu-encies.

3.4 Sometimes explicitly described as a "theatre" of cultural performance, festivals such the Smithsonian's Festival of American Folklife reframe (Goffman) sociocul-tural behaviors as staged enactments for a variety of ideological objectives, the foremost of which is cultural preservationism attempted through celebration, education, and validation (Whisnant 1979), an agenda with sociopolitical conno-tations (Whisnant 1983).

3.5 As a national cultural production that America presents to itself, the Festival of American Folklife is indeed a kind of living cultural theatre: it entails a staging of behaviors that rekeys the represented within the frame of the representation.

3.6 The Festival context brings about a juxtaposition of divergent frames of reference—that of the Smithsonian's production, that of the participants, and that of the audience.

3.7 Within this context, the presented sociocultural behaviors are rekeyed as *signs for* the authentic behaviors of specific social groups.

3.8 This transplantation of socially-situated behaviors to others' public and institu-tional frames—with some explicit or implicit directions to present and account for

ourself, your craft, your culture to total strangers in a setting contrived for more or
ss ideological reasons—affects the transplanted in several significant ways.

9 In the festival setting, the participant will have to do extra communicative
bor to contextualize, explain, present, and accomplish performance; the partici-
ant may also deliberately change performance according to perceived audience,
nticipated institutional intent, or individual objectives. Changes in repertory/
cipe and performance may also result from material limitations or the recom-
endations of Smithsonian fieldworkers or staff members.

10 Thus, in seeking to determine the effect that this rekeying has on traditional
erformance, we are also essentially concerned with the participants' framing of
e festival, and with the way these framings are manifest in their presentation of
lf, their representation of group, and in their recreation of tradition.

11 In addition to the immediate effects of the festival situation on presentations/
erformances, the Smithsonian Festival of American Folklife may also have a
sting effect on the participants, represented traditions, and the communities in
hich these have their social basis. Here, we are concerned with after-the-fact
aming and interpretation of event and experience by both participants and
embers of the community.

P P E N D I X II

uestions for Participants

4. Questions

1 BEFORE

1.1 *real people and their presentation:*
   what is your impression of the Festival of American Folklife? what do you
      think it is? what do you think its objectives are?
   are you having to make any special arrangements or changes in your usual
      schedule in order to make this trip?
   how do you feel about going?
   why do you want to go?
   does the honorarium offered by the Smithsonian make up for lost income?
   who is accompanying primary participant and why?
   how do you feel about going?

.2 *preparation/anticipation/self-presentation:*
   have you participated in a festival before?
   have you done this for any kind of public audience?
   do you teach/demonstrate/supervise others in this activity?
   what situation at home is closest to such a presentation—could we observe
      beforehand?

what preparations are you making for your "performance"?

what have you been told about what you are expected to do in FAF? by whom?

what do you anticipate—what to expect as far as setup, how to know what to present, what kinds of audience to expect?

any conflicts or objections?

4.1.3 *community reception:*

do other people in your community know you're going to participate in the FAF?

how did they find out—did you tell them, local newspaper, grapevine, etc.?

what are the reactions of the people at home to your participation in the festival?

how aware are people in your community of your involvement in the art or craft that you have been asked to come perform or demonstrate?

has your agreement to go to Washington made any change in this?

4.1.4 *decontextualization:*

are you concerned about presenting your art or craft in an unusual setting?

are you making any special preparations other than what you usually do (costumes, props, etc.) to suggest the appropriate atmosphere? (We need to be careful here not to put ideas or, especially, anxieties in their minds, since presumably the Smithsonian would have given specific directions if they expected the participants to be doing this.)

4.1.5 *work or everyday life as a display event:*

what do you feel like, being asked to perform for other than your usual audience or to turn your work into a performance?

who asked you if you wanted to participate (direct invitation from Smithsonian or through union leader, boss, band leader, etc.)?

what was your immediate reaction?

4.1.6 *self-image/re-presentation/re-creation:*

is this tradition still a central part of your community or family life? an ordinary day-to-day occurrence or reserved for special occasions?

do you see this practice dying out?

do you see self as a conscious preserver of tradition?

from whom did you learn?

do you do it differently than the person who taught you did? why or why not?

what do you see as your role at the festival?

what do you hope to accomplish?

why do you want to participate?

4.1.7 *from life to stage/reframing:*

has anyone asked or suggested that you emphasize the most traditional thing in your repertoire or otherwise alter your usual performance or practice?

do you anticipate having to do anything extra or different to make this make sense to the festival audience?

4.2 DURING

4.2.1 *real people and their presentation:*
since we talked to you at home in Michigan have you had to make any additional arrangements or changes in your usual schedule in order to make this trip?
how was the trip to Washington?
how was your reception here?
how are your living arrangements?
how do you feel about being here?
have you had a chance to see other parts of the festival and the Michigan exhibit? what do you think of them?
periodically throughout the festival—are you enjoying being here?
has anyone from your hometown or any friends or relatives come to see you here?
what do they think of what is going on and what you are doing?

4.2.2 *preparation/anticipation/self-presentation:*
(N.B. We should attend the Smithsonian briefing sessions for participants.)
what did the Smithsonian staff tell you in the orientation and workshop sessions?
before the festival actually begins—did the Smithsonian briefing or seeing the festival site or any other experience you've had since arriving in Washington change any of what you had expected?
are you making any last minute adaptations before the festival starts?
is this turning out to be what you had expected? if not, how is it different?
periodically throughout the festival—do you see yourself making any changes in your presentation? what are you doing differently? why?
is the audience responding to you as you would like?
if participant brought a companion—is it helpful to you to have someone else from home to talk to?

4.2.3 *decontextualization:*
how does the festival setting affect you (e.g., tents, outside, daytime, festival atmosphere instead of usual setting in VFW hall, workplace, own kitchen, etc.)?
what other things would normally be going on around you, at the same time? do you miss them?
would it give people a better picture if some of these could be represented, too?

4.2.4 *work or everyday life as a display event:*
now that you are actually here, what does it feel like to perform for this audience rather than your usual one or to perform your work as a display event?

4.2.5 *self-image/re-presentation/re-creation:*
(Building on what we learned of their self-identifications from previous interviews)
what do you see as your role at the festival?
what do you hope to accomplish?

why do you want to participate?

(Also notice at this stage the matter of language: does the participant play down or emphasize an ethnic or regional accent? how does audience respond? what does the audience appear to expect, a "folk" accent or Standard American English?)

4.2.6 *from life to stage/reframing:*

what aspects of your presentation or performance do the audiences like best? are these the newer or more traditional parts? are these the parts you think are most important?

how are things working out for you with your presenter?

what do you have to do extra or differently to make this make sense to the festival audience?

if participant teaches, organizes big dinners, or the like, how is this similar and different?

do you think you're getting through to people?

are there other things that you would like to be doing here, but can't because you didn't bring necessary materials?

(Also judge for ourselves at this stage:

is the person good at showing self/culture off?

is the presentation a success?)

4.2.7 *festival presentation as a sign of a sign:*

have you brought anything along from home to recreate the usual setting or atmosphere? are these things you usually have around or new creations meant to represent the setting?

4.2.8 *questions for person accompanying the main participant:*

what are your impressions of what is going on here?

how does the performer look or act differently from what you're used to in day to day contact?

how is the person you're accompanying adapting to the festival setting? has he/she expressed any concerns about being here to you? do you talk about plans for making the presentation work out well?

are you glad to be here, finding it a worthwhile way to spend some time?

have you had a chance to visit other parts of the festival? what do you think?

(N.B. also try to talk to other friends of the participant or people from his/her hometown if any come to visit—what do they think of the festival and of what the participant is doing?)

4.2.9 *questions for festival presenter:*

how is the presenting going? how are you getting along with the people for whom you are a presenter?

how well do you know the participants? the tradition being represented?

4.3 AFTER

4.3.1 *real people and their presentation:*

did you enjoy yourself?
was it worth the trouble?
would you do it again?
what did you get out of participating?
what and who did you enjoy most/least about the festival?
how were interactions with staff/audience/other participants?

.3.2 *preparation/anticipation/self-presentation:*
did what you were told beforehand prepare you adequately for participating?
what kinds of things would you have liked to know about in advance that
would have helped you be better prepared?
how are you preparing for the festival in East Lansing in August? have you
learned things from this experience that you will be applying here?

.3.3 *community reception:*
what do people around here think of your having participated in the festival?
are people more aware of you and what you do?
have you been contacted by more interested local learners or by more outside
buyers or enthusiasts?

.3.4 *decontextualization:*
in retrospect, do you think your performance or demonstration came off well?
could you communicate what you wanted to?
does it feel different now to do the same stuff back in the old settings?

.3.5 *work or everyday life as a display event:*
in retrospect, how do you feel about presenting your everyday activities as a
performance? did you enjoy doing it? what were FAF audiences like? how
were they different from your usual situation?
if participant had not formerly performed or sold craft commercially—do you
intend to do so now?

.3.6 *self-image/re-presentation/re-creation:*
has the experience of performing at the FAF changed your perspective of
yourself, the art or craft you do, or your relation to a local or extended
community?
do you do things differently now?

.3.7 *from life to stage/reframing:*
in retrospect, did the particular selection from your repertoire work out well
with the festival audience?
how did the presenting work out for you? do you prefer to talk about your
activity yourself, or discuss it with the presenter on stage or just do it and let
the presenter explain?

.3.8 *questions for the person who acccompanied the participant (if available):*
did you enjoy being at the festival?
do your impressions in retrospect match with those of the participant? if not,
how do your impressions differ?

4.4 AT THE MICHIGAN FESTIVAL

Most of the same questions from the "during" phase could apply. Our principal interests at this stage will be:

4.4.1 to collect the participants' impressions of how the two festival experiences are different, and

4.4.2 to attempt to judge for ourselves how adaptations made for the FAF have been carried over.

5. *Reflexivity*

5.1 Inevitably our study of the festival participants will add another degree of intervention, thus we need to ask ourselves:

5.1.1 *Before:* what effect is our additional presence having on the participants as they are preparing to go to Washington?
    are we just one more bother?
    have we increased their self-consciousness and/or preparation?
    is that a good or a bad thing?
    do they understand what our study is about and what do they think about it?
    what do those with whom Jongsung works think of being studied by a foreign student?

5.1.2 *During:* what effect is our additional presence here at the festival having on the participants?
    are they glad to have us around or sick of us?

5.2 We also need to be aware of our own practice as fieldworkers and how that may influence the data we collect:
    how much time are we actually spending with them? in an official or friendly capacity?
    are we mostly interviewing them in a fairly informal way or are we picking up the info we'd like to know indirectly through casual conversation?
    how often are we pressed into service to keep the festival running or to help out the performers instead of being detached researchers?
    in what position do we learn the most? are we combining information gathered in several different ways or relying mainly on one information-gathering system?
    how are we responding both to the specific person we're monitoring and to the whole experience?
    what can we suggest for future project design from our experiences?

Notes

1. The terminological distinctions have been and continue to be the subject of extensive debate, most of which is not germane here. See Bauman (1989) for a discussion of the principal issues. For the current mission statement of the Smithsonian Office of Folklike Programs, whose Festival of American Folklife is our focus, see Office of Folklife Programs, Smithsonian Institution (1988:6).

2. Exceptions include McCarl and Santino in Feintuch (1988) and Cadaval (1985). Only Cadaval's article was in print when we began this project.

3. We would like to offer our sincere thanks to Peter Seitel, Richard Kurin, Laurie Sommers, Tom Vennum, and virtually the entire staff of the Office of Folklife Programs for their support, assistance, and goodwill during the entire course of this project. Special thanks to Arlene Liebenau, who served as our liaison with the OFP.

4. Our work could not have proceeded without the kind assistance of many of those who did fieldwork for the Michigan program, including Kurt Dewhurst, Marsha MacDowell, Janet Gilmore, James Leary, Timothy Cochrane, Alan Cicala, Dennis Au, Yvonne Lockwood, Eliot Singer, Thomas Vennum, Jr., and Nicholas Spitzer, as well as Glenn Hinson, who recruited the North Carolina participants in the Language Conservation Program with whom we also worked.

5. Pseudonyms for the festival participants have been used throughout this report. Researchers and participants consulted are listed below:
Richard Anderson: Dave Ray, Gary Richards, Neil Charles, Will Ralston (Great Lakes fishermen)
Garry Barrow: the Simons (Old-time/Bluegrass musicians)
Inta Gale Carpenter: Karl Arnold (Ukrainian embroiderer), Steve Jayton, Will Davis (river guides, boat builders)
Patricia Sawin: Bob Jameson (wooden shoe maker), Harry and Polly Elder (muskrat cooks)
William Wheeler: Raymond Leslie (fiddle player), Lewis VanBuskirk (furniture maker)
Jongsung Yang: the Nowickis (Polish-American polka band), the Yemeni dancers

6. Notably Bauman with Louis Kettunen (member of the Finnish-American musical group Thimbleberry) and Carpenter with Phil Stephens (a county extension agent who demonstrated the culture and harvesting of cherries).

7. Especially teacher Hope Miller Lawson and ballad singer Rose Jenner.

8. The parallel with participants who made sense of unfamiliar festival activities by assimilating them to a familiar model is instructive.

9. Richard Anderson reported that Ray and Richards, who took to calling him "the spy," couldn't make much sense of what he was doing for our project or what a "folklore researcher" does, let alone how those two self-ascriptions might overlap. In field notes Anderson observed: "They can't seem to believe that I'm getting paid zip. Neither of them can understand why I want to get a Ph.D. and teach—'What good is it?'"

10. Pauley was eventually invited to the FAF and served both as a back-up musician for Leslie and as presenter.

11. Festival honoraria, for example, generally pay less than what people would make working at their jobs. While we estimated that two-thirds of the people with whom we worked were retired, the others had to take time off from work or close a private business in order to spend two weeks in Washington, or enlist the help of relatives to cover for them. Also, since the festival budget reimburses participants only for their own travel, participants who wanted to bring companions often spent most of their honorarium to accomplish that.

12. The orientation meeting the night before had described the walk through as the time to "check it out, make sure the space is right, make sure it feels and looks right and everything that you've requested be put in the area for you will be there." Those preparing the kitchen were behind schedule when the participants arrived, however, so the counters were dirty, the cupboards empty except for a few battered pots, and none of the specific utensils that the foodways participants had been asked to request and had requested were yet on site.

13. "The impression I conjured in my mind—initially—before anything was said, was that I would be in the Smithsonian buildings. Then when I find out I was outdoors—`OK, fine,' and in a tent—`OK, fine.' Then [only after arriving in D.C.] I find out I have this trellis thing—that I was supposed to mount embroidery on? . . . . I feel I was left in limbo without information I needed about displays. Set ups were gruelling because day in and day out I have to put up and take down, since it was outside and there was no security. Using pushpins and trying to be careful not to damage the threads" (Interview, 8-10-87).

14. In the North Carolina section of the Cultural Conservation program, Glenn Hinson devised a somewhat different presentation format. He provided extensive introductions, which included both a brief historical overview of the music and performance style and an in-depth discussion of music in the lives of the specific performers. He then remained on stage with the performers, asking questions and soliciting personal narratives and specific songs in order to make his points and to make transitions to the next performance. This style of presentation deemphasizes the music as entertainment and also elevates the presenter to a position of importance almost equal to that of the performers, which some may find problematic.

15. The commercial fishermen in particular resented recreational fishers and hunters because they feel beleaguered and discriminated against by the Department of Natural Resources in favor of the more lucrative tourist industry. While the differences between commercial and sport fishermen proved an ongoing source of tension, it is also important to note that participants themselves at times took the initiative to bridge this kind of gap. Janet Gilmore reports: "In a later session Rick Glimm, noticing Richards' antagonism towards him, admirably helped reduce tensions by taking a conciliatory tone in comparing his experiences with Richards'" (Gilmore, 4-27-89, p.5).

16. A news release about Michigan participants in the FAF entitled, "Some Things [or in some versions "Many Things"] Not as Expected" was an oft-repeated item in Michigan newspapers. The intent, in most instances, seems to have been to get a little partly humorous, partly self-congratulatory mileage out of showing that the bureaucrats in Washington, D.C. aren't too savvy about practical, country matters. The press appeal of this kind of feature, however, means that the kinds of small logistical problems endemic to festival could have larger repercussions in terms of broadcasting to local constituencies some of the troubles the participants faced.

References

Abrahams, Roger D. 1981. Shouting Match at the Border: The Folklore of Display Events, in Richard Bauman and Roger D. Abrahams, eds. *"And Other Neighborly Names": Social Process and Cultural Image in Texas Folklore*. Austin: University of Texas Press.

Bauman, Richard. 1977. *Verbal Art as Performance*. Prospect Heights, Illinois: Waveland Press.

——. 1986. *Story, Performance, and Event: Contextual Studies of Oral Narrative*. Cambridge: Cambridge University Press.

——. 1989. Folklore, in Erik Barnouw, ed., *International Encyclopedia of Communications*. Oxford: Oxford University Press.

—— and Patricia Sawin. 1991. The Politics of Participation in Folklife Festivals, in Ivan Karp and Steven D. Lavine, eds., *Exhibiting Culture: The Poetics and Politics of Museum Display*. Washington, D.C.: Smithsonian Institution Press.

Cadaval, Olivia. 1985. "The Taking of the Renwick": The Celebration of the Day of the Dead and the Latino Community of Washington, D.C. *Journal of Folklore Research* 22:179–93.

Camp, Charles, and Timothy Lloyd. 1980. Six Reasons Not to Produce a Folk Festival. *Kentucky Folklore Record* 26:67–74.

Cantwell, Robert. 1991a. Conjuring Culture: Ideology and Magic in the Festival of American Folklife. *Journal of American Folklore* 104:148–63.

——. 1991b. Response to Peter Seitel. *Journal of American Folklore* 104:496–99.

Carey, George. 1976. The Storyteller's Art and the Collector's Intrusion, in Linda Dégh, Henry Glassie, Felix J. Oinas, eds., *Folklore Today: A Festschrift for Richard M. Dorson*. Bloomington: Research Center for Language and Semiotic Studies.

Feintuch, Burt, ed. 1988. *The Conservation of Culture: Folklorists and the Public Sector*. Lexington: The University Press of Kentucky.

Feld, Steven. 1987. Dialogic Editing: Interpreting How Kaluli Read *Sound and Sentiment*. *Cultural Anthropology* 2:190–210.

Fine, Elizabeth C. 1984. *The Folklore Text: From Performance to Print*. Bloomington: Indiana University Press.

Goffman, Erving. 1974. *Frame Analysis: An Essay on the Organization of Experience*. New York: Harper Colophon.

Goody, Esther, ed. 1978. *Questions and Politeness*. Cambridge: Cambridge University Press.

Kirshenblatt-Gimblett, Barbara. 1988. Mistaken Dichotomies. *Journal of American Folklore* 101:140–55.

——. 1991. Objects of Ethnography, in Ivan Karp and Steven D. Lavine, eds., *Exhibiting Cultures: The Poetics and Politics of Museum Display*. Washington, D.C.: Smithsonian Institution Press.

Kurin, Richard. 1991. Cultural Conservation through Representation: Festival of India Folklife Exhibitions at the Smithsonian Institution, in Ivan Karp and Steven D. Lavine, eds., *Exhibiting Culture: The Poetics and Politics of Museum Display*. Washington, D.C.: Smithsonian Institution Press.

MacCannell, Dean. 1976. *The Tourist*. New York: Schocken Books.

Office of Folklife Programs. 1988. *1988 Festival of American Folklife Program Book*. Washington, D.C.: Smithsonian Institution.

Mudimbe, V. Y. 1988. *The Invention of Africa*. Bloomington: Indiana University Press.

Mullen, Patrick G. 1981. A Traditional Storyteller in Changing Contexts, in Richard Bauman and Roger D. Abrahams, eds., *"And Other Neighborly Names": Social Process and Cultural Image in Texas Folklore*. Austin: University of Texas Press.

Paredes, Américo. 1977. On Ethnographic Work Among Minority Groups. *New Scholar* 6:1–32.

Samarin, William J. 1967. *Field Linguistics*. New York: Holt, Rinehart and Winston.

Sawin, Patricia E. 1988. The 1987 Smithsonian Festival of American Folklife: An Ethnography of Participant Experience. Bloomington, Ind.: Folklore Institute, manuscript.

Schechner, Richard. 1985. Restoration of Behavior, in *Between Theater and Anthropology*. Philadelphia: University of Pennsylvania Press.

Seitel, Peter. 1991. Magic, Knowledge, and Irony in Scholarly Exchange: A Comment on Robert Cantwell's Observations on the Festival of American Folklife. *Journal of American Folklore* 104:495–96.

Spitzer, Nicholas R. 1987. *Presenter's Guide: 1987 Festival of American Folklife*. Unpublished, Office of Folklife Programs, Smithsonian Institution.

Stoeltje, Beverly J. 1989. Festival, in Erik Barnouw, ed., *International Encyclopedia of Communications*. Oxford: Oxford University Press.

Whisnant, David E. 1983. *All That Is Native and Fine: The Politics of Culture in an American Region*. Chapel Hill: University of North Carolina Press.

——— . 1979. *Folk Festival Issues*, JEMF Special Series No. 12. Los Angeles: University of California Press.

About the Team

Left to right: Jongsung, Will, Dick, Patricia, Richard, Inta, and Garry

IN 1990 RICHARD ANDERSON moved to Japan to become curator for the Ikegami Honmoniji Temple, which is the largest Buddhist temple complex in Tokyo. He completed his doctoral studies at the Folklore Institute in 1988 with a dissertation on Taiken: Personal Narratives and Japanese New Religions." In 1987, GARRY W. BARROW accepted a position as State Folklife Coordinator for the Virginia Folklife Program at the Virginia Foundation for the Humanities and Public Policy. He is a doctoral candidate in folklore. RICHARD BAUMAN is Distinguished Professor of Folklore and Anthropology at Indiana University, Bloomington. His most recent book is *Folklore, Cultural Performances, and Popular Entertainments* (1992). INTA GALE CARPENTER continues as Associate Director of Special Projects at the Folklore Institute, but in 1990 was also appointed Assistant Research Scholar at Indiana University. She completed her Ph.D. in 1989 with a dissertation on Latvian exile folklore as ideology. PATRICIA SAWIN now lives in Chapel Hill, North Carolina. She is teaching folklore in area colleges as she finishes her dissertation on a topic she identified during the 1987 FAF project—the performance of self and tradition in the life of an Appalachian woman. WILLIAM W. WHEEELER is writing his dissertation while living in Mansfield, Pennsylvania. His topic is the relationship between practice and improvisation in flamenco music. JONGSUNG YANG, a performer and teacher of Korean folk dance in his own right, is in Korea pursuing dissertation research on the designation of cultural properties as "Living National Treasures."

Reflections on the Folklife Festival:
An Ethnography of Participant Experience
was designed by Matthew S. Williamson (text)
and Dennis Hill (cover), with typesetting by CompuType,
Bloomington. The text was composed in 9/13 Stone Serif
with Stone Sans Serif display. The book was printed offset
by Cushing-Malloy, Inc., Ann Arbor, Michigan, on 70 lb.
Matte text stock and 80 lb. Beckett Concept cover stock.